Microsoft Excel 2013
Master Class

Michelle N. Halsey

ISBN-10: 1-64004-121-4
ISBN-13: 978-1-64004-121-9

Contents

Chapter 1 – Opening Excel

Welcome to the new and improved Microsoft Excel 2013. This chapter will teach you how to open Microsoft Excel files and create new ones. First, we will learn how to open Microsoft Excel. You will learn how to open files from the Recent list or other files. Then you will learn how to create a blank workbook or a workbook from a template.

Opening Excel

To open Excel in Windows 8, use the following procedure.

Step 1: From the Start page, select the Excel 2013 icon.

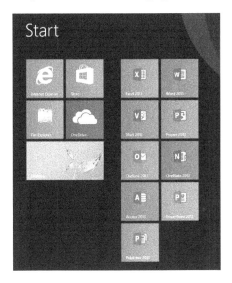

Use this procedure if using Windows 7:

Step 1: Select the Start icon from the lower left side of the screen.

Step 2: Select **All Programs**.

Step 3: Select **Microsoft Office**.

Step 4: Select **Microsoft Office Excel 2013**.

Using the Recent List

To open a workbook from the Recent list, use the following procedure.

Step 1: Select the workbook that you want to open from the Recent list.

To pin an item on the Recent list, use the following procedure.

Step 1: Click the pin on the right side of the Recent list item. The item moves to the top section of the Recent list.

To unpin an item, click the pin on the right side of the Recent list again. The item returns to the previous location in the Recent list.

Opening Files

To open a workbook, use the following procedure.

Step 1: Select **Open Other Workbooks** from the bottom of the Recent list. Or select **Open** from the Backstage View.

Step 2: Select one of the **Places** you would like to look for the workbook. The default options are Recent Workbooks, your Microsoft SkyDrive location, and your Computer.

13

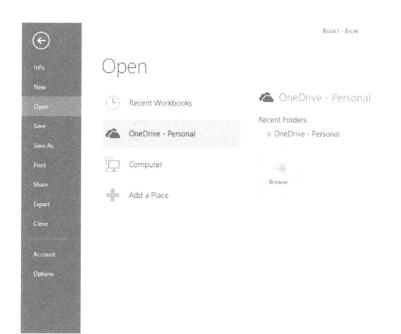

Step 3: To open a document from the SkyDrive or your computer, select **Browse**.

Step 4: In the *Open* dialog box, navigate to the location of the file you want to open. Select it and select **Open**.

Creating a Blank Workbook

To create a blank workbook, use the following procedure.

Step 1: If the Backstage view is not showing, select the **File** tab from the Ribbon. Select **New**.

Step 2: From the **New** tab, or if you have just opened Excel 2013, select **Blank Workbook**.

Creating a Workbook from a Template

To create a blank workbook from a template, use the following procedure.

Step 1: If the Backstage view is not showing, select the **File** tab from the Ribbon. Select **New**.

Step 2: From the **New** tab, or if you have just opened Excel 2013, select the template you want to use.

Step 3: Select **Create**.

You can use the left and right arrows to review the other templates in the current search.

To search for a template and filter the results, use the following procedure.

Step 1: Select one of the Suggested Search terms or enter a term in the Search box and press Enter.

Step 2: To apply a filter, select the Filter term from the list on the right side of the screen.

Step 3: To return to the list of templates, select **Home**.

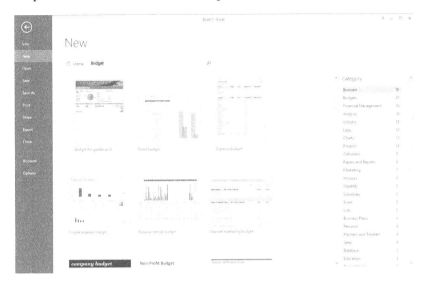

Chapter 2 – Working with the Interface

In this chapter, we will introduce you to the Excel 2013 interface, which uses the Ribbon from the previous two versions of Excel. You will get a closer look at the Ribbon and the Status bar. You will also learn how to manage your Microsoft account right from a new item above the Ribbon. This chapter introduces you to the Backstage view, where all of the functions related to your files live. You will learn how to save files. Finally, we will look at closing files and closing the application.

Understanding the Interface

Explore the Excel interface, including the Ribbon, the formula bar, the worksheet area, the Quick Access toolbar, and the Status bar.

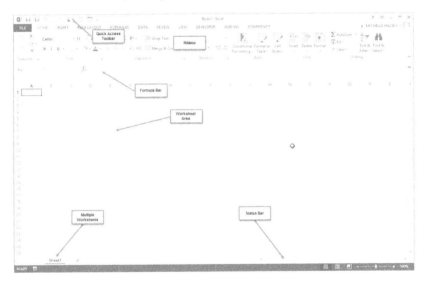

Each Tab in the Ribbon contains many tools for working with your workbook. To display a different set of commands, click the Tab name. Buttons are organized into groups according to their function.

The Quick Access toolbar appears at the top of the Excel window. It provides you with one-click shortcuts to commonly used functions, like save, undo, and redo.

We will discuss the Formula bar more in Chapter 6.

The Status bar shows if any macros are currently running. It also allows you to quickly change your view or zoom of the workbook.

To zoom in or out, use the following procedure.

Step 1: Click the minus sign in the Status bar to zoom out. Click the plus sign in the Status bar to zoom in. You can also drag the slider to adjust the zoom.

You can also click on the number percentage to open the *Zoom* dialog box.

About Your Account and Feedback

Explore the account options, use the following procedure.

Step 1: Click on the arrow next to the name to change the photo, open the profile information, see the account setting for the current user, or to sign in as a different user.

To send feedback to Microsoft, use the following procedure.

Step 1: Select the Smile icon at the top right corner of the screen.

Step 2: Select Send a Smile or Send a Frown.

Step 3: Enter the information requested in the Microsoft Office Feedback dialog. Select **Send**.

Using Backstage View

Explore the Backstage View, use the following procedure.

Step 1: Select the **File** tab on the Ribbon.

Excel displays the Backstage View, open to the Info tab by default. A sample is illustrated below.

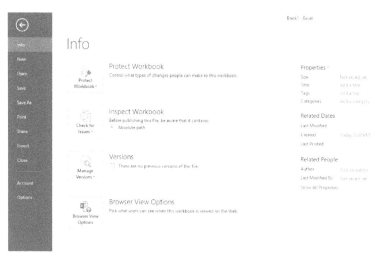

Understanding Worksheets

To move the active cell, point out the highlighted row and column for the active cell, as well as the name of that cell in the Name box.

To insert a new worksheet, use the following procedure.

Step 1: Click the **New Sheet** plus sign.

Excel opens the new worksheet to the first cell, so that you can begin entering data right away. You can rename the worksheet if needed.

To rename a worksheet, use the following procedure.

Step 1: Right click on the sheet tab and select **Rename** from the context menu.

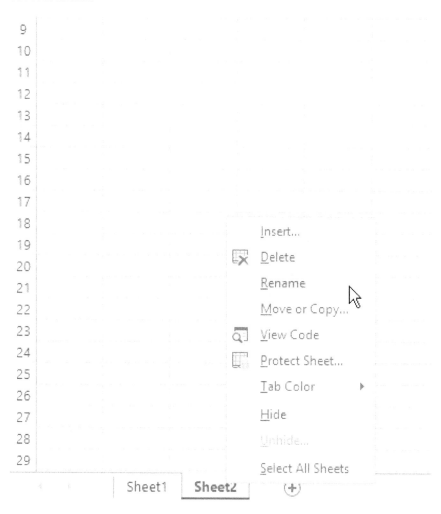

Step 2: Enter the new name over the highlighted text.

To switch to a different worksheet, use the following procedure.

Step 1: Click on the worksheet tab that you want to view.

To move a worksheet, use the following procedure.

Step 1: Click on the worksheet tab that you want to move and drag it to the new location in the workbook.

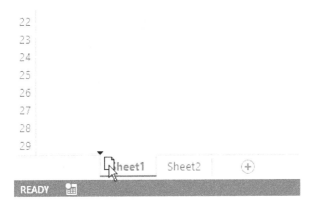

Saving Files

To save a workbook that has not been previously saved, use the following procedure.

Step 1: Select the **File** tab on the Ribbon.

Step 2: Select the **Save** command in the Backstage View.

Step 3: Select the **Place** where you want to save the workbook.

Step 4: If you choose your SkyDrive, you can select the **Documents** folder. If you choose your Computer, select your **Current Folder** or one of your **Recent Folders**. Or in either place, you can choose **Browse** to select a new location.

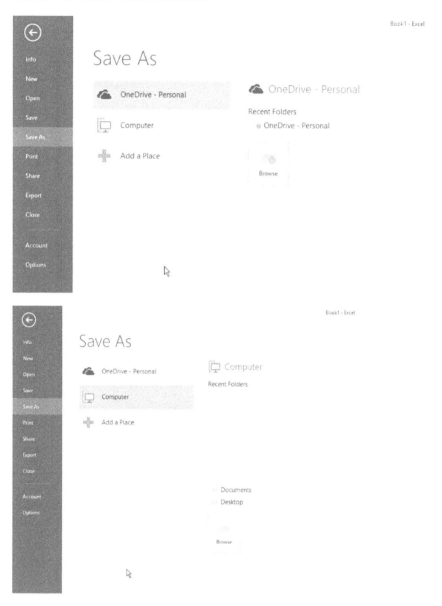

Step 5: The *Save As* dialog opens. Enter a **File Name**, and if desired, navigate to a new location to store the file. Select **Save**.

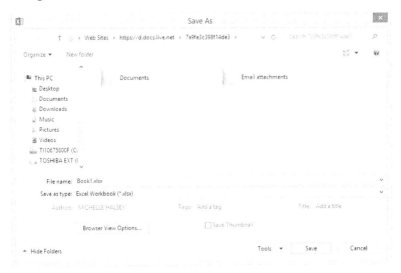

Closing Files vs. Closing Excel

To close a file, use the following procedure.

Step 1: Select the **File** tab from the Ribbon.

Step 2: Select **Close** from The Backstage View.

If you have not saved your file, you will see the following message.

To close the application (if only one workbook is open), use the following procedure.

Step 1: Click the X at the top right corner of the window.

Chapter 3 – Your First Worksheet

In this chapter, you will start entering data into a worksheet, including using flash fill and auto fill to quickly populate the information you need to store in your worksheet. You will also learn about editing data, including checking your spelling. Since you probably do not want to move all of those rows or columns when you realize that you forgot one, you will also learn how to add rows and columns.

Entering Data

Review how a long label will overlap to the next column. In the following example, "Car Payment" is too long for the column width.

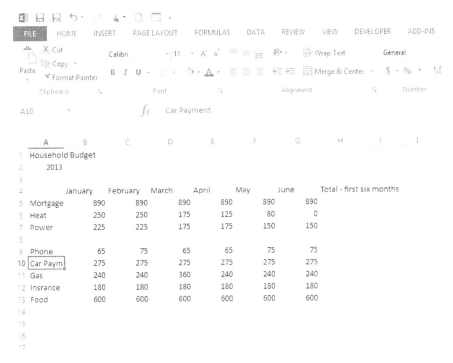

	A	B	C	D	E	F	G	H	I	J
1	Household Budget									
2	2013									
3										
4		January	February	March	April	May	June	Total - first six months		
5	Mortgage	890	890	890	890	890	890			
6	Heat	250	250	175	125	80	0			
7	Power	225	225	175	175	150	150			
8										
9	Phone	65	75	65	65	75	75			
10	Car Paym	275	275	275	275	275	275			
11	Gas	240	240	360	240	240	240			
12	Insrance	180	180	180	180	180	180			
13	Food	600	600	600	600	600	600			
14										
15										
16										
17										

To widen a column, use the following procedure.

Step 1: Click on the column you want to widen. Notice the cursor changes to a cross with double arrows. The screen tips indicate how wide in pixels the column currently is.

Step 2: Drag the border to the new width

Using Auto Fill

To create a list using AutoFill, use the following procedure. This example creates new columns in the Budget worksheet to cover the second six months.

Step 1: Create a new column heading with the text "July" in cell J4.

Step 2: Select that cell to make it active. Excel displays a handle around the cell.

Step 3: Drag the handle across the columns. Excel displays a screen tip showing what AutoFill will place in those cells.

Step 4: Release the mouse button at the end of the range.

Editing Data

Explore the relationship between the active cell and the Formula Bar.

Checking Your Spelling

Explore the Spell Checker, use the following procedure.

Step 1: Select the **Spelling** tool on the **Review** tab of the Ribbon.

Excel opens the **Spelling** dialog box and begins indicating any spelling errors.

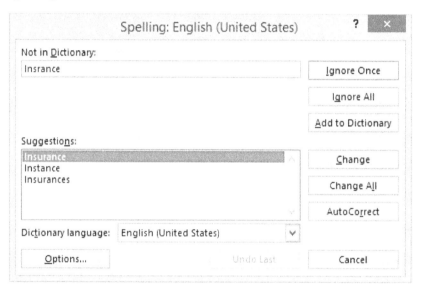

Step 2: Highlight the correct spelling and select Change. If the correct spelling is not listed, you can correct the spelling by editing the text in the **Not in Dictionary** field.

Adding Rows and Columns

To add a new row, use the following procedure.

Step 1: Highlight the row below where you want to insert a row. Click to the left of the row number to highlight the whole row.

Step 2: Select **Insert Sheet Rows** from the Ribbon.

Using Flash Fill

To use flash fill, use the following procedure.

Step 1: Enter Nancy in the First Name cell of the first row.

Step 2: Enter Andrew in the First Name cell of the second row.

Step 3: When Excel displays the remaining list, press Enter to accept.

Step 4: Notice the icon that appears with a context menu of additional options.

Chapter 4 – Viewing Excel Data

Excel offers several options for viewing your worksheets. This chapter will provide an overview of the different views that are available. It also explains how to switch views and create a custom view. This chapter covers how to use the Zoom feature. Finally, this chapter discusses how to switch between different open files.

An Overview of Excel's Views

Explain the different view options in Excel.

- Normal is the view used for entering data.

- Page Break Preview allows you to adjust where the page breaks occur. You can drag the blue border to a new location for columns or rows to adjust the page breaks.

- Page Layout view displays what the data will look like when printed. You can use Page Layout view to add headers and footers to your worksheets.

Explore the **View** tab on the Ribbon.

Explore the view options on the Status bar.

Switching Views

Explore the Page Break Preview, use the following procedure.

Step 1: Select the **View** tab from the Ribbon.

Step 2: Select the **Page Break Preview** tool.

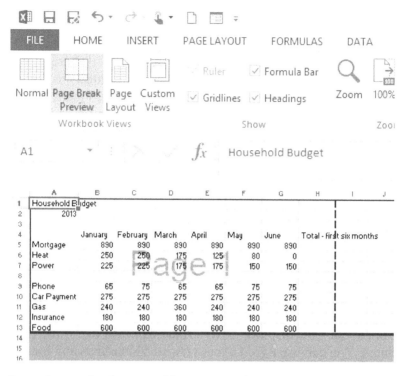

Investigate what happens if you move the blue borders.

Explore the Page Layout View, use the following procedure.

Step 1: Select the **View** tab.

Step 2: Select the **Page Layout** tool.

There are three areas for the header and the footer. Practice entering header content in the left, middle, and right of the header and/or footer.

Using Zoom

To zoom to a selection, use the following procedure.

Step 1: Highlight the area you want to view larger.

Step 2: Select the **Zoom to Selection** tool from the **View** tab on the Ribbon.

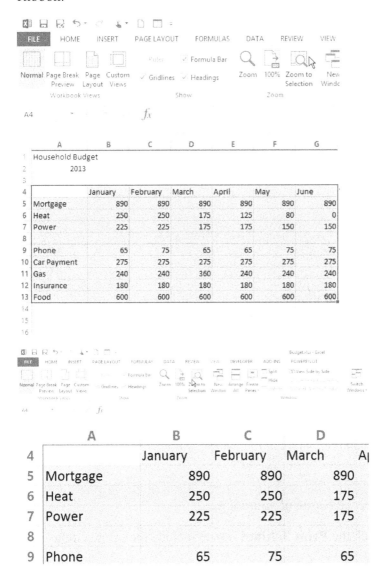

Step 3: Select **100%** from the View tab on the Ribbon to return to the default zoom.

Creating Custom Views

To create a custom view, use the following procedure.

Step 1: Select **Custom Views** from the **View** tab on the Ribbon.

Excel opens the *Custom Views* dialog box.

Step 2: Select **Add** to open the *Add View* dialog box.

Step 3: Enter the **Name** of your view.

Step 4: Check the **Print Settings** box to include the print settings in your custom view.

Step 5: Check the **Hidden rows, columns and filter settings** to include those in your custom view.

Step 6: Select **OK**.

To apply a custom view, use the following procedure.

Step 1: Select **Custom Views** from the **View** tab on the Ribbon.

Step 2: Highlight the View you want to apply and select **Show**.

Switching Between Open Files

To switch from one worksheet to another, use the following procedure.

Step 1: Select the **Switch Windows** tool from the **View** tab on the Ribbon. Select the worksheet you want to view from the list.

Chapter 5 – Building Formulas

The backbone of Excel is its ability to perform calculations. There are two ways to set up calculations in Excel: using formulas or using functions. Formulas are mathematical expressions that you build yourself. You need to follow proper math principles in order to obtain the expected answer. Building the formula is simply a matter of combining the proper cell addresses with the correct operators in the right order. This chapter will explore how to build, edit, and copy formulas. This chapter will also explain the difference between relative and absolute references. Finally, this chapter will explain how to use the Status Bar to perform simple calculations. We will explore functions in the next chapter.

The Math Basics of Excel

Review the different types of operators.

The Arithmetic operators are:

- Plus Sign (+) – Adds values
- Minus Sign (-) – Subtracts values
- Asterisk (*) – Multiplies values
- Forward slash (/) – Divides values
- Percent sign (%) – Finds the percentage of a value
- Caret (^(– Exponentiation – Finds the exponential value

The Comparison operators are:

- Equals (=) sign – Equates values
- Greater than (>) sign – Indicates that one value is greater than the other
- Less than sign (<) – Indicates that one value is less than the other
- Greater than or equal to (>=) signs – Indicates that one value is greater than or equal to the other
- Less than or equal to (<=) signs – Indicates that one value is less than or equal to the other
- Not Equal (<>) – Indicates that values are not equal

Text concatenation allows you to combine text from different cells into a single piece of text. The operator is the **&** sign.

The reference operators combine a range of cells to use together in an operation. The reference operators are:

- Colon (:) – A Range operator that produces a reference to all of the cells between the references on either side of the colon
- Comma (,) – A Union operator that combines multiple range references
- Space – An intersection operator that returns a reference to the cells common to the ranges in the formula

Building a Formula

To enter a formula to calculate the Total Value in the sample worksheet, use the following procedure.

Step 1: Select the Total Value column for the first product (cell D4).

Step 2: Enter the = sign to begin the formula.

Step 3: Select cell B4 to use it as the first value in the formula. Excel enters the reference as part of the formula.

Step 4: Enter the * sign.

Step 5: Click on cell C4 to use it as the second value in the formula. Excel enters the references as part of the formula.

Step 6: Press **ENTER** to complete the formula. Excel moves to the next row and performs the calculations in the formula.

The following illustration shows the answer to the calculation in the cell, and since the cell is active, you can see the formula in the Formula bar.

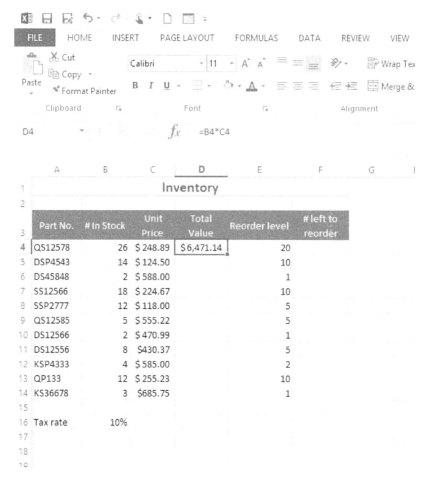

Cell reference: D4 | fx | =B4*C4

Inventory					
Part No.	# In Stock	Unit Price	Total Value	Reorder level	# left to reorder
QS12578	26	$ 248.89	$ 6,471.14	20	
DSP4543	14	$ 124.50		10	
DS45848	2	$ 588.00		1	
SS12566	18	$ 224.67		10	
SSP2777	12	$ 118.00		5	
QS12585	5	$ 555.22		5	
DS12566	2	$ 470.99		1	
DS12556	8	$430.37		5	
KSP4333	4	$ 585.00		2	
QP133	12	$ 255.23		10	
KS36678	3	$685.75		1	
Tax rate	10%				

Editing a Formula

To edit a formula, use the following procedure. The following example uses an incorrect cell reference in a formula.

Step 1: Select the cell with the formula you want to correct to make it active.

Step 2: Select the Formula Bar. Excel highlights the cell references in the current formula.

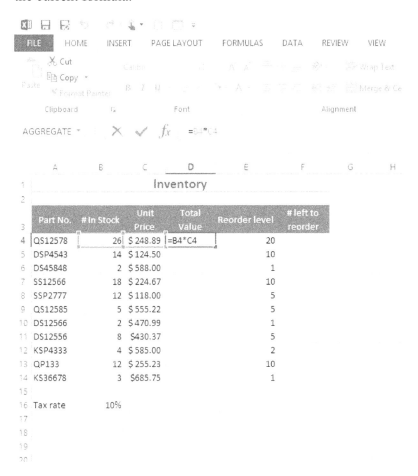

Step 3: Highlight the operator or cell references and either type over with the correct reference or operator, or select the correct cell to replace a cell reference.

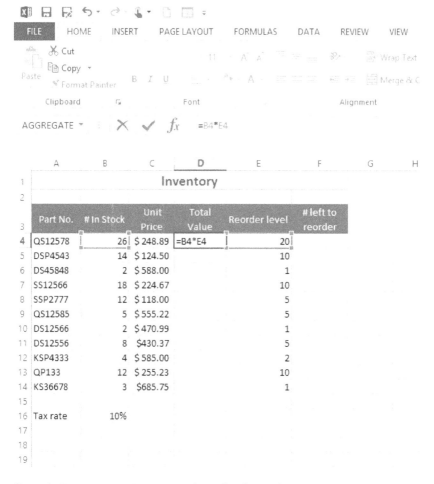

Step 4: Press ENTER to complete the formula. Excel calculates the formula and moves to the next row.

Copying a Formula

To copy and paste a formula, use the following procedure.

Step 1: Select the cell with the formula you want to copy. You can also click on the cell and use the keyboard shortcut: **CTRL + C**.

Step 2: Select **Copy** from the **Home** tab on the Ribbon.

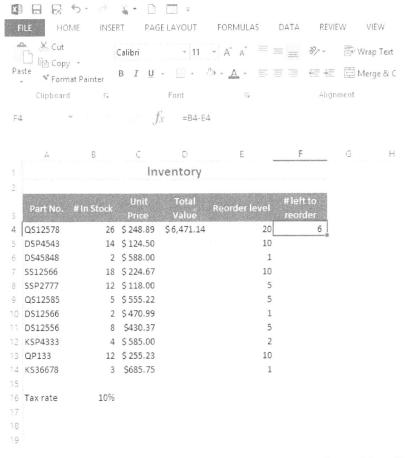

| | FILE | HOME | INSERT | PAGE LAYOUT | FORMULAS | DATA | REVIEW | VIEW |

Calibri · 11 · A˙ A˙ Wrap Text
B *I* U · · A · Merge & C
Cut Copy Format Painter
Paste
Clipboard Font Alignment

F4   *fx*   =B4-E4

	A	B	C	D	E	F	G	H
1				Inventory				
2								
3	Part No.	# In Stock	Unit Price	Total Value	Reorder level	# left to reorder		
4	QS12578	26	$ 248.89	$ 6,471.14	20	6		
5	DSP4543	14	$ 124.50		10			
6	DS45848	2	$ 588.00		1			
7	SS12566	18	$ 224.67		10			
8	SSP2777	12	$ 118.00		5			
9	QS12585	5	$ 555.22		5			
10	DS12566	2	$ 470.99		1			
11	DS12556	8	$430.37		5			
12	KSP4333	4	$ 585.00		2			
13	QP133	12	$ 255.23		10			
14	KS36678	3	$685.75		1			
15								
16	Tax rate	10%						
17								
18								
19								

Excel highlights the cell whose contents you are copying. This will remain highlighted until you finish pasting, in case you want to paste the cell contents more than once.

Select the cell where you want to copy the formula. Excel displays a number of paste options. To paste a formula, select **Paste** or **Paste formula**. Note that as you hover your mouse over the paste options, the rest of the context menu is dimmed. You can also select the cell and use the keyboard shortcut: **CTRL + V**.

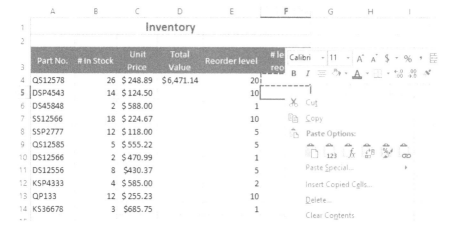

Part No.	# In Stock	Unit Price	Total Value	Reorder level	# le reo
QS12578	26	$ 248.89	$6,471.14	20	
DSP4543	14	$ 124.50		10	
DS45848	2	$ 588.00		1	
SS12566	18	$ 224.67		10	
SSP2777	12	$ 118.00		5	
QS12585	5	$ 555.22		5	
DS12566	2	$ 470.99		1	
DS12556	8	$430.37		5	
KSP4333	4	$ 585.00		2	
QP133	12	$ 255.23		10	
KS36678	3	$685.75		1	

Step 1: You can repeat the paste as many times as desired. Or you can highlight multiple cells at once before pasting to repeat the paste for all highlighted cells.

Step 2: Press **ENTER** to stop pasting.

Relative vs. Absolute References

To copy a formula with an absolute reference, use the following procedure.

Step 1: Create a new column labeled Taxes.

Step 2: Select the Taxes column for the first product (cell E4).

Step 3: Enter the = sign to begin the formula.

Step 4: Select cell B16 to use it as the first value in the formula. Excel enters the reference as part of the formula. Use the Formula Bar to enter dollar signs before the column and the row (i.e., $B$16).

Step 5: Enter * and the relative reference in the Total Value column.

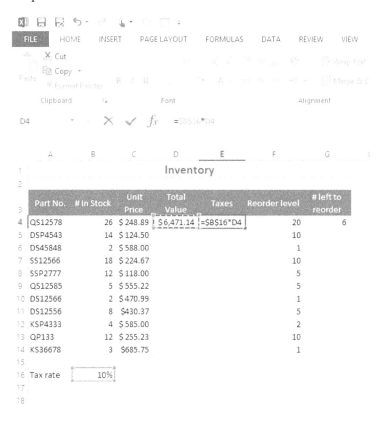

Step 6: Press **ENTER** to complete the formula. Excel moves to the next row and performs the calculations in the formula.

Copy the formula for the other products and select some of them to see the results.

Using the Status Bar to Perform Calculations

To customize the Status Bar, use the following procedure.

Step 1: Right click on the Status Bar to see a list of Functions that can be displayed. For this example, select MIN and MAX.

Step 2: Press **ESC** or click elsewhere in the worksheet to close the **Customize Status Bar** list.

Explore the calculations performed when you highlight a group of cells.

	A	B	C	D	E	F	G	H	I
4		January	February	March	April	May	June	Total - first six months	
5	Mortgage	890	890	890	890	890	890		
6	Heat	250	250	175	125	80	0		
7	Power	225	225	175	175	150	150		
8									
9	Phone	65	75	65	65	75	75		
10	Car Payment	275	275	275	275	275	275		
11	Gas	240	240	360	240	240	240		
12	Insurance	180	180	180	180	180	180		
13	Food	600	600	600	600	600	600		
14									
15									
16									

Chapter 6 – Using Excel Functions

This chapter introduces Excel functions, which are a little like templates for common formulas. There are many different types of functions. First, we will look at the SUM function. You will learn about using AutoComplete for entering formulas. We will look at other basic common functions as well. We will take a look at the Formulas tab introduced in the Ribbon for Excel 2007. Finally, we will take a look at the function names.

Formulas vs. Functions

To open the Insert Function dialog box, use the following procedure.

Step 1: Select the **Insert Function** tool right next to the Formula Bar.

Investigate the different categories and functions in the *Insert Function* dialog box. Point out the bottom part of the screen where the syntax and description of the function appear.

Using the SUM Function

Review how to use a SUM function to add the total for each category in the sample file, use the following procedure.

Step 1: Select the Total –First Six Months column for the first category (cell H5).

Step 2: Select the **AutoSum** tool in the Editing Group on the **Home** tab of the Ribbon.

Step 3: Excel enters the function with a default selection of the cell references you want to use in the function highlighted.

AGGREGATE ▾   ✕ ✓ *fx*   =SUM(B5:G5)

	A	B	C	D	E	F	G	H	I	J
1	Household Budget									
2	2013									
3										
4		January	February	March	April	May	June	Total - first six months		
5	Mortgage	890	890	890	890	890	890	=SUM(B5:G5)		
6	Heat	250	250	175	125	80	0	SUM(number1, [number2], ...		
7	Power	225	225	175	175	150	150			
8										
9	Phone	65	75	65	65	75	75			
10	Car Payment	275	275	275	275	275	275			
11	Gas	240	240	360	240	240	240			
12	Insurance	180	180	180	180	180	180			
13	Food	600	600	600	600	600	600			
14										
15										
16										
17										

Step 4: If the cell references are not accurate, you can drag the highlighted area to include additional cells or remove cells you do not want used in the function.

Step 5: Press **ENTER** to complete the function.

Excel performs the calculation and moves to the next row. In the following illustration, the cell with the function is active, so that you can see the function syntax in the Formula Bar and the result in the cell.

	A	B	C	D	E	F	G	H
1	Household Budget							
2	2013							
3								
4		January	February	March	April	May	June	Total - first six months
5	Mortgage	890	890	890	890	890	890	5340
6	Heat	250	250	175	125	80	0	
7	Power	225	225	175	175	150	150	
8								
9	Phone	65	75	65	65	75	75	
10	Car Payment	275	275	275	275	275	275	
11	Gas	240	240	360	240	240	240	
12	Insurance	180	180	180	180	180	180	
13	Food	600	600	600	600	600	600	
14								
15								

Using AutoComplete

To use the AutoComplete feature, use the following procedure.

Step 1: Begin typing the SUM function. As soon as you type the Equals sign and the letter S, Excel displays a possible list of matching functions.

Step 2: To select the SUM Function from the list, double-click on the SUM function.

Step 3: Excel enters the function, but you must still enter the arguments. You can simply click on multiple cells, or click and drag to select a cell range. You can also type in the cell references.

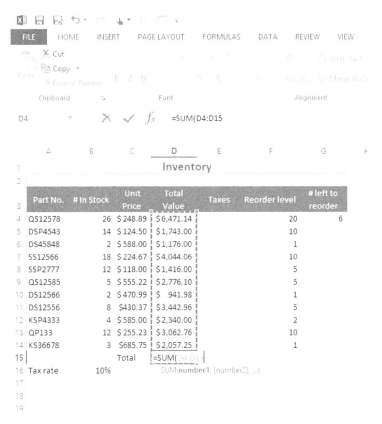

Step 4: Enter the final parenthesis mark to end the function.

Step 5: Press ENTER to enter the function in the cell.

Using Other Basic Excel Functions

Review how to use the AVERAGE function as an example of another function, use the following procedure.

Step 1: Add a new label in column I: Average.

Step 2: Select the cell in the Average column for the first category.

Step 3: Select the arrow next to the SUM function on the Home tab of the Ribbon to see the list of other common functions.

Step 4: Select **Average**.

Excel enters the function with the most likely cell references.

	January	February	March	April	May	June	Total - first six months	Average
5 Mortgage	890	890	890	890	890	890	5340	=AVERAGE(B5:H5)
6 Heat	250	250	175	125	80	0		AVERAGE(number1, [number2], ...)
7 Power	225	225	175	175	150	150		
8								
9 Phone	65	75	65	65	75	75		

Step 5: Replace the cell references so that cell H5 is not included in the average.

	January	February	March	April	May	June	Total - first six months	Average
5 Mortgage	890	890	890	890	890	890	5340	=AVERAGE(B5:G5)
6 Heat	250	250	175	125	80	0		AVERAGE(number1, [number2], ...)
7 Power	225	225	175	175	150	150		
8								
9 Phone	65	75	65	65	75	75		

Step 6: Press **ENTER** to complete the function.

Understanding the Formulas Tab

Explore the **Formulas** tab on the Ribbon.

Understanding Function Compatibility

Explore the icons that appear when entering a function name. The old names have a yellow warning triangle next to them.

=beta

Chapter 7 – Using Quick Analysis

The new Quick Analysis tools allow you to easily preview and apply a number of formatting, charts, totals, tables, and spark lines features to your data. We will first look at the formatting tools. You will also learn about the recommended charts available in Quick Analysis. Next, we will look at the totals tools that include formulas that automatically calculate totals for you. We will also look at the tables available with Quick Analysis. Once you have your data in table format, you can use a number of sorting and filtering tools, which we will also discuss in this chapter. Finally, you will learn how to create spark lines.

Formatting Data

To apply Quick Analysis formatting, use the following procedure.

Step 1: Select the table (A1 to D16) in the sample worksheet.

Step 2: Select the icon that appears at the bottom right of the table.

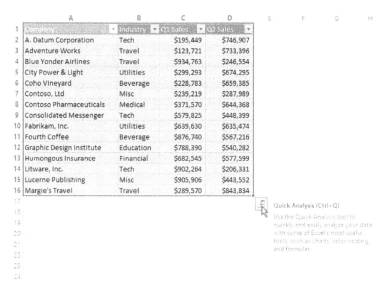

	A	B	C	D
1	Company	Industry	Q1 Sales	Q2 Sales
2	A. Datum Corporation	Tech	$195,449	$746,907
3	Adventure Works	Travel	$123,721	$733,396
4	Blue Yonder Airlines	Travel	$934,763	$246,554
5	City Power & Light	Utilities	$299,293	$674,295
6	Coho Vineyard	Beverage	$228,783	$659,385
7	Contoso, Ltd	Misc	$239,219	$287,989
8	Contoso Pharmaceuticals	Medical	$371,570	$644,368
9	Consolidated Messenger	Tech	$579,825	$448,399
10	Fabrikam, Inc.	Utilities	$639,630	$635,474
11	Fourth Coffee	Beverage	$876,740	$567,216
12	Graphic Design Institute	Education	$788,390	$540,282
13	Humongous Insurance	Financial	$682,545	$577,599
14	Litware, Inc.	Tech	$902,264	$206,331
15	Lucerne Publishing	Misc	$905,906	$443,552
16	Margie's Travel	Travel	$289,570	$843,834

Quick Analysis (Ctrl-Q)

Use the Quick Analysis tool to quickly and easily analyze your data with some of Excel's most useful tools, such as charts, color-coding, and formulas.

Step 3: Select the formatting type that you want to use.

Step 4: For the **Greater Than** option (and some other types of options), enter the cell that contains the value to which you want to compare the others. You can also enter a number or a formula. Also select the formatting you want to use from the drop down list.

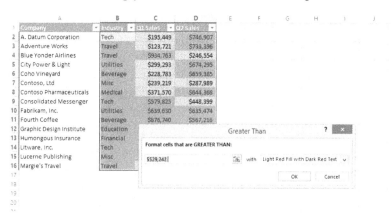

To remove any formatting you have applied, select **Clear format**.

Creating Quick Analysis Charts

To create Quick Analysis charts, use the following procedure.

Step 1: Select the table (A1 to D16) in the sample worksheet.

Step 2: Select the icon that appears at the bottom right of the table.

Step 3: Select **Charts**.

Step 4: Select the chart type that you want to use.

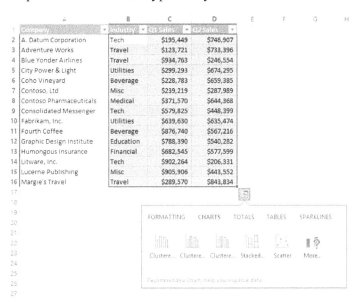

The chart is inserted into your worksheet. If the chart you selected is a PivotChart, it will be created on a separate worksheet.

Calculating Totals

To create Quick Analysis totals, use the following procedure.

Step 1: Select the table (A1 to D16) in the sample worksheet.

Step 2: Select the icon that appears at the bottom right of the table.

Step 3: Select **Totals**.

Step 4: Select the formula that you want to use. Note that there is a right arrow to view additional options.

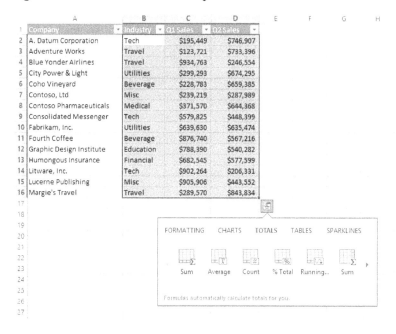

The row or column you selected is inserted into your worksheet.

Creating Quick Analysis Tables

To create Quick Analysis tables, use the following procedure.

Step 1: Select the table (A1 to D16) in the sample worksheet.

Step 2: Select the icon that appears at the bottom right of the table.

Step 3: Select **Tables**.

Step 4: Select the table type that you want to use.

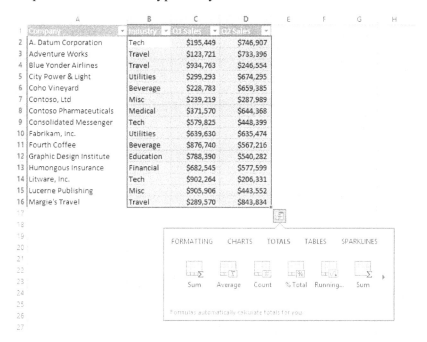

The Table is inserted into your worksheet with formatting and filtering options activated. If the table you selected is a PivotTable, it will be created on a separate worksheet.

Sorting and Filtering Your Data

To sort, use the following procedure.

Step 1: Select the arrow next to the column header that you want to use for sorting or filtering. Or you can select the **Sort & Filter** tool from the Ribbon.

Step 2: Select a sorting option from the list. The list differs, depending on the type of data in the column you selected.

To create a custom sort, use the following procedure.

Step 1: Select one column header you want to use in your sort.

Step 2: Select the **Sort & Filter** tool from the Ribbon.

Step 3: Select **Custom Sort**.

Excel opens the *Sort* dialog box.

Step 4: You can choose the first column by which to sort from the **Sort By** drop down list. The options displayed match the column headers in your worksheet.

Step 5: Select an option from the **Sort On** drop down list. **Values** is selected by default.

Step 6: Select an **Order** from the drop down list.

Step 7: To add another column to your sort, select **Add Level**. Repeat steps 4, 5, and 6 for the next sorting level. You can **Delete the Level**, **Copy a Level**, and rearrange the order of the sorting levels by using the up or down arrows.

Step 8: Select **OK** when you have finished setting up your sort to see the results.

To apply a simple filter, use the following procedure.

Step 1: Select the arrow next to the column header for the column including the value you want to filter.

Step 2: To select a simple filter based on your type of data, select the option provided above the search box. In the example, below, select **Number Filters**. Then select the filter you want to use from the list. Excel will display a dialog box to determine the value to use in your filter.

Step 3: Enter the value you want to use in the dialog box and select **OK**.

Step 4: To select a simple filter based one or more of your specific values, clear the **Select All** check box to clear the boxes. Check one or more boxes from the items that are taken from your data. Select **OK** to apply the filter.

Excel includes a different small icon in the column header to indicate that a filter has been applied. It only shows the rows that match the filter. The other rows are still present, but hidden.

C	D
Q1 Sales	Q2 Sales
$934,763	$246,554
$579,825	$448,399
$639,630	$635,474
$876,740	$567,216
$788,390	$540,282
$682,545	$577,599
$902,264	$206,331
$905,906	$443,552

To clear a filter, use the following procedure.

Step 1: Select the Filter icon next to the column header to open the Sort and Filter context menu.

Step 2: Select **Clear Filter From** to clear the filter.

Using Spark Lines

To create Quick Analysis spark lines, use the following procedure.

Step 1: Select the table (A1 to D16) in the sample worksheet.

Step 2: Select the icon that appears at the bottom right of the table.

Step 3: Select **Spark lines**.

Step 4: Select the type of mini chart that you want to use.

Chapter 8 – Formatting Your Data

In this chapter, we will look at how to make your worksheet more appealing by changing the font type and size, alignment, formatting numbers, and by adding color and borders. This chapter also explains how to use the merge feature and how to remove formatting.

Changing the Appearance of Text

To apply formatting to text, use the following procedure.

Step 1: Select one or more cells that you want to format.

Step 2: Right-click to display the context menu, or use the formatting tools on the **Home** tab.

Step 2a: Use the **Font** drop down list to select a new font for the text.

Step 2b: Use the **Font Size** drop down list to select a new font size for the text. Alternatively, you can use the **Increase Font Size** or **Decrease Font Size** tools to adjust the font size a point at a time.

Step 2c: Select **Bold, Italics,** or **Underline** to add these features to your text.

Changing the Appearance of Numbers

To format a number as currency without decimals, use the following procedure.

Step 1: Select the cell or cell range that you want to format.

Step 2: Select the type of number formatting you want to use from the **Number** group drop down list in the **Home** tab of the Ribbon.

Step 3: Select the Decrease Decimal tool (2 times) to remove the decimal places.

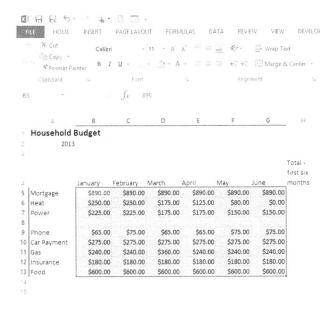

Adding Borders and Fill Color

To add borders, use the following procedure.

Step 1: Highlight the cell or cell range where you want to apply your border.

Step 2: Select the type of border you want to apply from the **Borders** tool on the **Home** tab of the Ribbon.

To apply fill colors, use the following procedure.

Step 1: Highlight the cell or cell range where you want to apply your fill color.

Step 2: Select the color you want to apply from the **Fill Color** tool on the **Home** tab of the Ribbon.

Removing Formatting

To clear formatting, use the following procedure.

Step 1: Select the cell or cell range that you want to clear.

Step 2: Select the **Clear** tool from the **Home** tab on the Ribbon.

Step 3: Select **Clear Formats**.

Working with Alignment Options

To align cell contents, use the following procedure.

Step 1: Select the cell or cell range that you want to align.

Step 2: Select the type of alignment you want to use from the Alignment group tools in the Home tab of the Ribbon.

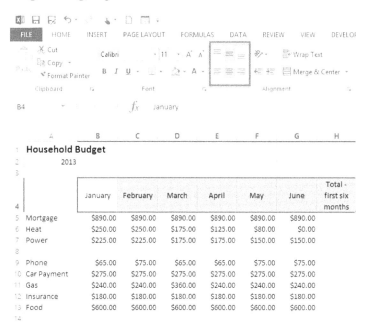

	January	February	March	April	May	June	Total - first six months
Household Budget							
2013							
Mortgage	$890.00	$890.00	$890.00	$890.00	$890.00	$890.00	
Heat	$250.00	$250.00	$175.00	$125.00	$80.00	$0.00	
Power	$225.00	$225.00	$175.00	$175.00	$150.00	$150.00	
Phone	$65.00	$75.00	$65.00	$65.00	$75.00	$75.00	
Car Payment	$275.00	$275.00	$275.00	$275.00	$275.00	$275.00	
Gas	$240.00	$240.00	$360.00	$240.00	$240.00	$240.00	
Insurance	$180.00	$180.00	$180.00	$180.00	$180.00	$180.00	
Food	$600.00	$600.00	$600.00	$600.00	$600.00	$600.00	

To merge cells, use the following procedure.

Step 1: Highlight the cell range that you want to merge.

Step 2: Select the **Merge** tool from the **Home** tab of the Ribbon.

Step 3: Select **Merge & Center**.

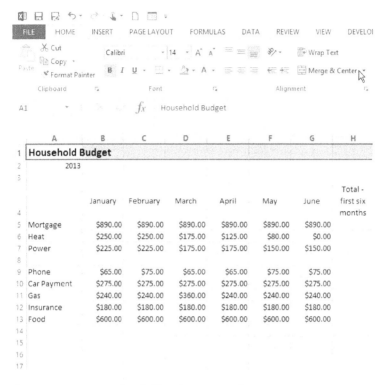

To wrap text, use the following procedure.

Step 1: Select the cell that you would like to wrap.

Step 2: Select **Wrap Text** from the **Home** tab on the Ribbon.

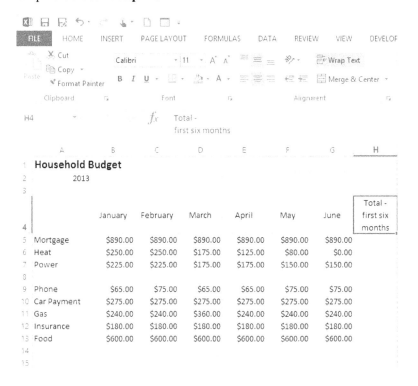

	A	B	C	D	E	F	G	H
1	**Household Budget**							
2	2013							
3								
4		January	February	March	April	May	June	Total - first six months
5	Mortgage	$890.00	$890.00	$890.00	$890.00	$890.00	$890.00	
6	Heat	$250.00	$250.00	$175.00	$125.00	$80.00	$0.00	
7	Power	$225.00	$225.00	$175.00	$175.00	$150.00	$150.00	
8								
9	Phone	$65.00	$75.00	$65.00	$65.00	$75.00	$75.00	
10	Car Payment	$275.00	$275.00	$275.00	$275.00	$275.00	$275.00	
11	Gas	$240.00	$240.00	$360.00	$240.00	$240.00	$240.00	
12	Insurance	$180.00	$180.00	$180.00	$180.00	$180.00	$180.00	
13	Food	$600.00	$600.00	$600.00	$600.00	$600.00	$600.00	
14								
15								

Chapter 9 – Using Styles, Themes, and Effects

In this chapter, you will learn some more advanced formatting options. First, we will discuss table styles and cell styles, including using the *Format Cells* dialog box to apply all types of formatting to your cells at once. This chapter explains conditional formatting. You have seen a little conditional formatting with the Quick Analysis formats. Conditional formatting is simply applying a certain type of formatting to cells that meet certain requirements. Finally, you will learn how to change the theme, colors and fonts, which can help you provide a consistent branding to all of your documents, workbooks, and other office creations.

Using Table Styles and Cell Styles

To apply a table style, use the following procedure.

Step 1: Highlight the cell or cell range where you want to apply your style.

Step 2: Select the **Format as Table** arrow from the **Home** tab on the Ribbon to see the gallery of options.

Step 3: Select the style that you want to apply.

Step 4: In the *Format as Table* dialog box, Excel shows the cell range for your table matching your selection. If you need to change it, you can select a new range of cells. Check the **My Table has Headers** box if applicable. Select **OK**.

The data is now formatted as a table, with filtering options in the column headers.

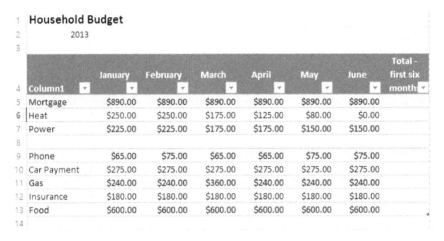

		January	February	March	April	May	June	Total – first six month
4	Column1							
5	Mortgage	$890.00	$890.00	$890.00	$890.00	$890.00	$890.00	
6	Heat	$250.00	$250.00	$175.00	$125.00	$80.00	$0.00	
7	Power	$225.00	$225.00	$175.00	$175.00	$150.00	$150.00	
8								
9	Phone	$65.00	$75.00	$65.00	$65.00	$75.00	$75.00	
10	Car Payment	$275.00	$275.00	$275.00	$275.00	$275.00	$275.00	
11	Gas	$240.00	$240.00	$360.00	$240.00	$240.00	$240.00	
12	Insurance	$180.00	$180.00	$180.00	$180.00	$180.00	$180.00	
13	Food	$600.00	$600.00	$600.00	$600.00	$600.00	$600.00	

To apply a cell style, use the following procedure.

Step 1: Highlight the cell or cell range where you want to apply your style.

Step 2: Select the **Cell Styles** tool from the **Home** tab of the Ribbon to see the style gallery.

Step 3: Select the style that you want to apply. You can see a preview before you select a style.

To create a new cell style, use the following procedure.

Step 1: Highlight the cell or cell range where you want to apply your style.

Step 2: Select the Cell Styles tool from the Home tab of the Ribbon to see the style gallery.

Step 3: Select **New Cell Style** to open the Style dialog box.

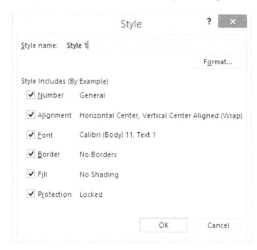

Step 4: Enter a name for the style in the **Style Name** field.

Step 5: Check the **Style Includes** boxes to indicate what formatting features the style should include.

Step 6: Select **Format** to open the **Format Cells** dialog box.

Step 7: Use the *Format Cells* dialog box to indicate each formatting feature for the style. Select **OK** when you have finished indicating all of the formatting features for the style.

Step 7a: The **Number** tab allows you to set number formatting for cells that contain values.

Step 7b: The **Alignment** tab allows you to set text alignment for cells that contain text.

Step 7c: The **Font** tab allows you to set the font for the style.

Step 7d: The **Border** tab allows you to set customized borders for the style.

Step 7e: The **Fill** tab allows you to set customized fill color for the style.

Step 7f: The **Protection** tab allows you to protect the cells from changes if you use the Protection feature.

Step 8: Select **OK** to save your style and close the *Style* dialog box.

The new style appears at the top of the Cell Style gallery.

Using Conditional Formatting

To apply conditional formatting, use the following procedure. In this example, we will format all monthly totals in the budget that are over $2500.

Step 1: Highlight the cell or cell range where you want to use conditional formatting.

Step 2: Select the **Conditional Formatting** tool from the **Home** tab on the Ribbon.

Step 3: Select **Highlight Cell Rules**. Select **Greater Than**.

Excel displays the *Greater Than* dialog box to help you complete the conditional formatting rule.

Step 4: Enter 2500 in the left field.

Step 5: Select a formatting option from the right drop down list.

Step 6: Select **OK** to apply the conditional formatting.

	A	B	C	D	E	F	G	H
1	**Household Budget**							
2	2013							
3								
4		January	February	March	April	May	June	Total - first six months
5	Mortgage	890	890	890	890	890	890	5340
6	Heat	250	250	175	125	80	0	880
7	Power	225	225	175	175	150	150	1100
8								0
9	Phone	65	75	65	65	75	75	420
10	Car Payment	275	275	275	275	275	275	1650
11	Gas	240	240	360	240	240	240	1560
12	Insurance	180	180	180	180	180	180	1080
13	Food	600	600	600	600	600	600	3600
14		2725	2735	2720	2550	2490	2410	15630
15								

To create a new conditional formatting rule, use the following procedure.

Step 1: Highlight the cell or cell range where you want to use conditional formatting.

Step 2: Select the **Conditional Formatting** tool from the **Home** tab on the Ribbon.

Step 3: Select **New Rule**.

Excel opens the **New Formatting Rule** dialog box.

Step 4: The options in this dialog box differ, based on the **Rule Type** you select. Select the **Rule Type** and follow the prompts to indicate the conditions for when to apply the formatting.

Step 5: Select **Format** to open the **Format Cells** dialog box to create the formatting to apply when the conditions are met.

Step 6: Select **OK** to save your rule and close the **New Formatting Rule** dialog box.

Changing the Theme, Colors, and Fonts

To change the theme, use the following procedure.

Step 1: Select the **Page Layout** tab from the Ribbon.

Step 2: Select **Themes**.

Step 3: Select a new theme from the gallery. You can see a preview of each theme before you apply it.

To change the colors, use the following procedure.

Step 1: Select the **Page Layout** tab from the Ribbon.

Step 2: Select **Colors**.

Step 3: Select a new color scheme from the gallery. You can see a preview of each color scheme before you apply it.

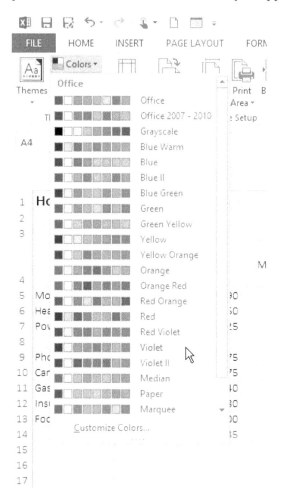

To change the fonts, use the following procedure.

Step 1: Select the **Page Layout** tab from the Ribbon.

Step 2: Select **Fonts**.

Step 3: Select a new font scheme from the gallery. You can see a preview of each font scheme before you apply it.

Chapter 10 – Printing and Sharing Your Workbook

This chapter discusses printing your worksheets. First, the chapter covers the Page Layout tab for setting up the worksheet page. Next, the chapter goes into more detail on setting up your pages. The chapter discusses how to use Print Preview. Finally, the chapter explains how to print your worksheets.

An Overview of the Page Layout Tab

Explore the **Page Layout** tab on the Ribbon.

Setting up Your Page

To change the page orientation, use the following procedure.

Step 1: Select the **Page Layout** tab from the Ribbon.

Step 2: Select **Orientation**.

Step 3: Select **Landscape**.

To use custom margins, use the following procedure.

Step 1: Select **Custom Margins** from the **Margins** tool on the **Page Layout** tab of the Ribbon.

Excel displays the *Page Setup* dialog box.

Step 2: Use the up and/or down arrows to control each of the margins (in inches). When have finished, select **OK**.

To insert a page break, use the following procedure.

Step 1: Place your cursor on the row or column where you want the page break to occur. Excel will insert the break above and to the left of your cursor.

Step 2: Select the **Breaks** tool from the **Page Layout** tab on the Ribbon.

Step 3: Select **Insert Page Break**.

Explore the **Print** tab in the Backstage View.

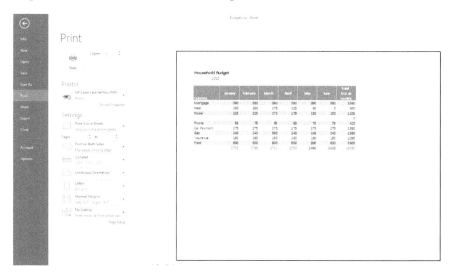

Inviting People

To invite people to the workbook, use the following procedure.

Step 1: Select the **File** tab from the Ribbon to open the Backstage view.

Step 2: Select the **Share** tab.

Step 3: Select **Invite People**.

Step 4: Enter the names or email addresses for the people that you want to invite.

Step 5: Enter a message to include with the invitation.

Step 6: If desired, check the **Require User To Sign-In Before Accessing Document** box to enhance the security of your workbook.

Step 7: Select **Share**.

To get a link for the document, use the following procedure.

Step 1: Select the **File** tab from the Ribbon to open the Backstage view.

Step 2: Select the **Share** tab.

Step 3: Select **Get a Link**.

Step 4: Select the **Create Link** button next to **View Link** or **Edit Link** (or both), depending on what type of editing rights you want to provide. You can copy the link and paste it to another location, such as an email or a blog page.

Step 5: If you want to remove the sharing rights, select **Disable Link**.

E-Mailing Your Workbook

To email an attachment or send a link, use the following procedure.

Step 1: Select the **File** tab on the Ribbon.

Step 2: Select the **Share** tab in the Backstage View.

Step 3: Select **Email**.

Step 4: Select **Send as Attachment** or **Send a Link**.

Step 5: Outlook opens with an email started.

If you select **Send as Attachment**, the name of the document is used as the subject and the document is already attached to the email. Enter the email addresses and any personal message you want to include.

If you select **Send a Link**, the name of the document is used as the subject and the link is included in the body message of the email. Enter the email addresses and any personal message that you want to include.

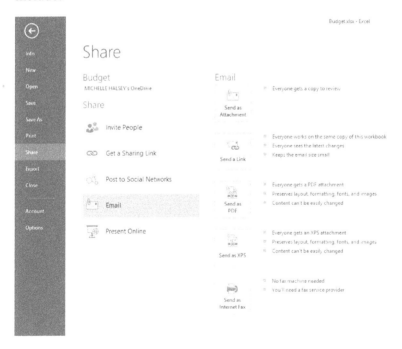

Chapter 11 – Smart Art and Objects

SmartArt, pictures, text boxes, and shapes are different ways to enhance your spreadsheet, especially when sharing the information with others. In this chapter, we will look at how to add these objects to your spreadsheets. We will also look at how to edit a SmartArt diagram. Finally, you will learn about the contextual Tools tabs that appear in Excel 2013 when you are working with different types of objects.

Inserting SmartArt

To insert SmartArt, use the following procedure.

Step 1: Select the Insert tab from the Ribbon.

Step 2: Select SmartArt.

Step 3: In the Choose a SmartArt Graphic dialog box, select the category on the left. Then you select the item in the middle. The right shows a preview of the item. Select OK to insert the content.

Excel inserts the selected SmartArt graphic in the middle of the spreadsheet.

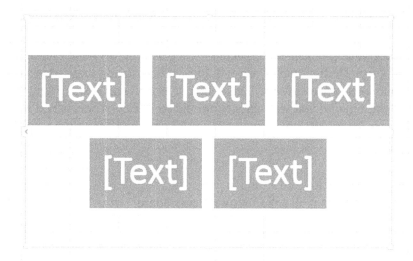

You can simply click on one of the boxes and type in your text, if desired. Notice that the font sizes adjust, depending on how much text you enter.

To add text to a SmartArt graphic using the Text pane, use the following procedure.

Step 1: To the left of the SmartArt graphic you inserted, there is a small rectangle with an arrow. Click this arrow to open the Text Pane.

Excel opens the Text Pane.

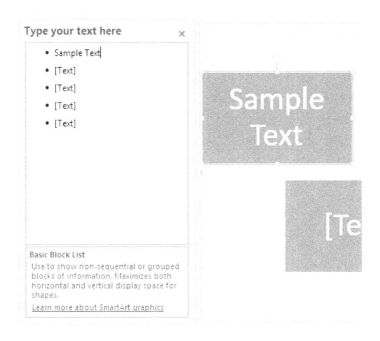

Step 2: Click on the first line and begin typing. Each line represents a new item in the graphic.

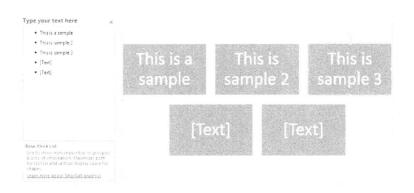

The SmartArt text adjusts to fit the graphic. The more text you enter in each graphic element, the smaller the text will become.

Step 3: When you have finished, click anywhere on the spreadsheet, and the Text Pane will close automatically. Or you can click the X in the top right corner.

To resize a SmartArt graphic, use the following procedure.

Step 1: Select the SmartArt graphic to select it. Notice the border around the graphic.

Step 2: Select one of the corners and drag the picture. Notice the cursor changes to a diagonal line with arrows at both ends. You can make it smaller or bigger, depending on which direction you drag.

Step 3: Release the mouse when the graphic is the desired size. Notice that Excel may rearrange the graphic elements for the best look and fit.

To move the diagram, use the following procedure.

Step 1: Select the diagram border.

The cursor changes to a cross with four arrows.

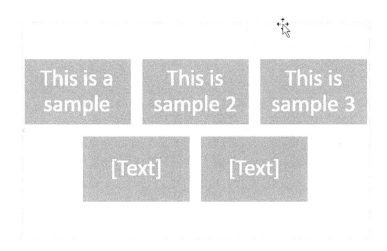

Step 2: Drag the mouse to move the diagram. Release the mouse when the diagram is in the desired location.

Note that you can move the individual parts of the SmartArt diagram using the same procedure. Just click on the individual object you want to move. Practice this for the next segment of the lesson.

Resetting the diagram allows you to quickly return the graphic to the original alignment and spacing between elements, use the following procedure to reset a diagram.

Step 1: Right-click on the diagram.

Step 2: Select Reset Graphic from the context menu.

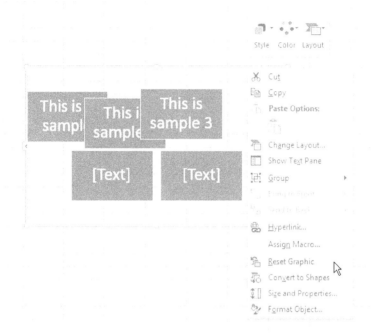

Adding Pictures

To insert a picture from a file, use the following procedure.

Step 1: Select the Insert tab from the Ribbon.

Step 2: Select Picture.

Step 3: Navigate to the location of the file and highlight the file you want to insert.

Step 4: Select Insert.

Excel inserts the picture.

To insert an online picture, use the following procedure.

Step 1: Select the Insert tab from the Ribbon.

Step 2: Select Online Pictures.

Step 3: In the **Insert Pictures** dialog box, select the place where you want to search for images.

Step 4: Enter a search term. Press Enter to begin searching.

Step 5: Excel displays the matching images. To insert one, double-click it or highlight it and select Insert.

To insert a full size screenshot, use the following procedure.

Step 1: Select the Insert tab from the Ribbon.

Step 2: Select Screenshot.

Step 3: The Screenshot gallery includes a thumbnail image of other windows you have open. Select the image that you want to insert.

Excel inserts the image.

To insert a screen clipping, use the following procedure.

Step 1: Make sure that the area of the screen you want is ready to capture. Excel will automatically return to the previous window for a screen clipping.

Step 2: Select the Insert tab from the Ribbon.

Step 3: Select Screenshot.

Step 4: Select Screen Clipping.

Step 5: Drag the mouse to capture the area of the screen that you want to insert in your presentation. The screen is slightly greyed out, except for the area you are capturing.

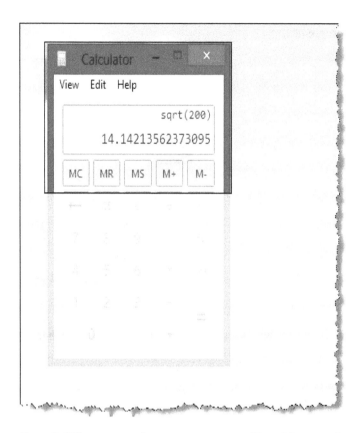

Step 6: When you release your mouse, Excel inserts the screen clipping into the workbook at the current cursor position.

Adding Text Boxes

To insert a text box, use the following procedure.

Step 1: Select the Insert tab from the Ribbon.

Step 2: Select Text Box. Select Horizontal Text Box or Vertical Text Box.

Step 3: Click on the worksheet and drag the mouse to draw the text box.

Step 4: When you release the mouse, Excel inserts the text box.

Step 5: Begin typing to enter text into the text box.

Drawing Shapes

To draw a shape, use the following procedure.

Step 1: Select the Insert tab from the Ribbon.

Step 2: Select Shapes.

Excel displays the Shapes gallery.

Step 3: Select a shape tool.

Step 4: Drag the mouse in the desired location to create the selected shape. The cursor is a cross while you are drawing.

Step 5: Release the mouse to complete the shape.

About the Contextual Tabs

The Tools tabs for working with SmartArt.

The Tools tab for working with pictures.

The Tools tab for working with a Text box or shape.

Chapter 12 – Auditing

This chapter introduces concepts that will help you troubleshoot formulas as we progress through the course. Precedent cells are cells whose contents are used in the active cell. Dependent cells are used in other cells contents or formulas. This chapter explains how to show these relationships. It also explains how to display the formulas, instead of the results, in a worksheet. You will also learn how to work with comments in this chapter.

Tracing Precedent Cells

To trace precedents, use the following procedure.

Step 1: Select the cell that contains the formula you want to trace. Cell D18 is used in this example.

Step 2: Select the Formulas tab from the Ribbon.

Step 3: Select Trace Precedents.

Step 4: Excel adds a tracer arrow from each cell that provides data to the active cell.

Line Item	February	March
PROFIT AND LOSS		
Revenue		
Budget	$75,000	$85,000
Actual	$70,000	$88,000
Budget variance (Actual – Budget)	($5,000)	$3,000
Prior year	$60,000	$70,000
Prior year variance (Actual – Prior year)	$10,000	$18,000
Cost of Goods Sold		
Budget	$55,000	$65,000

To remove the tracers, select Remove Arrows.

Tracing the Dependents of a Cell

To trace dependents, use the following procedure.

Step 1: Select the cell that you want to trace. Cell D18 is used in this example.

Step 2: Select the Formulas tab from the Ribbon.

Step 3: Select Trace Dependents.

Step 4: Excel adds a tracer arrow to each cell that uses the active cell's data.

Step 5: Click the Trace Dependents tool again to see further relationships that are influenced by the active cell's contents.

Line Item	February	March	Q1	April
PROFIT AND LOSS				
Revenue				
Budget	$75,000	$85,000	$225,000	$75,00
Actual	$70,000	$88,000	$218,000	$95,00
Budget variance (Actual – Budget)	($5,000)	$3,000	($7,000)	$20,00
Prior year	$60,000	$70,000	$185,000	$75,00
Prior year variance (Actual – Prior year)	$10,000	$18,000	$33,000	$20,00
Cost of Goods Sold				

Displaying Formulas Within the Sheet

To display formulas within the sheet, use the following procedure.

Step 1: Select the Formulas tab from the Ribbon.

Step 2: Select Show Formulas.

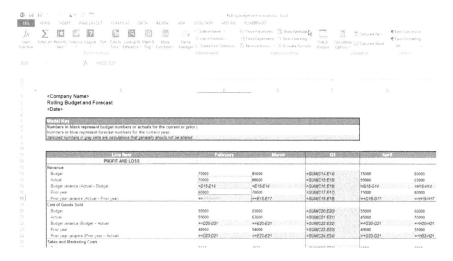

Excel expands the cells as necessary and displays all the worksheet's formulas in their cells.

Adding, Displaying, Editing, and Removing Comments

To add a comment, use the following procedure.

Step 1: Select the cell where you want to add a comment.

Step 2: Select the Review tab from the Ribbon.

Step 3: Select New Comment.

Step 4: Begin typing your comment.

	Q1	April	May
	$225,000	$75,000	$80,000
	$218,000	$95,000	$65,000
)	($7,000)		
	$185,000	Sample Comment|	
year)	$33,000		
	$170,000	$55,000	$60,000
	$165,500	$45,000	$55,000
)	$4,500	$10,000	$5,000
	$147,000	$49,000	$51,000
.ctual)	($18,500)	$4,000	($4,000)

To show or hide comments, use the following procedure.

Step 1: Select the cell with the comment.

Step 2: Select Show/Hide Comment or Show All Comments.

To edit a comment, use the following procedure.

Step 1: Select the cell with the comment.

Step 2: Select Edit Comment.

Excel opens the comment for editing. You can select text to change it, delete, or add text to the comment.

Q1	April	May	Ju
$225,000	$75,000	$80,000	$90,
$218,000	$95,000	$65,000	$88,
($7,000)	Sample Comment		($2,
$185,000			$90,
$33,000			($2,
$170,000	$55,000	$60,000	$70,
$165,500	$45,000	$55,000	$63,

To remove a comment, use the following procedure.

Step 1: Select the cell with the comment.

Step 2: Select Delete from the Review tab on the Ribbon.

Chapter 13 – Creating Charts

Charts provide a visual way of relating information. We will start with a new feature in 2013: Recommended Charts. Excel provides a customized set of charts based on data you select. This chapter will also explain how to insert a chart of your choosing. You will learn about the chart tools tab and gain an overview of the parts of a chart. Finally, you will learn how to resize and move a chart.

Using Recommended Charts

To insert a recommended chart, use the following procedure.

Step 1: Select the data that you want to use in your chart.

Step 2: Select the Insert tab from the Ribbon.

Step 3: Select Recommended Charts.

Step 4: In the **Insert Chart** dialog box, the Recommended Charts tab shows several charts that Excel recommended for the type of data you have selected. As you select each option on the left side of the dialog box, the right side shows a preview.

Step 5: When you find a chart that you want to use, select it in the list, and select OK.

Inserting a Chart

The types of charts in Excel 2013 are:

Column charts – Column charts allow you to visually compare values across a few categories.

Line Chart – Line charts show trends over time (such as years, months, or days) or categories.

Pie charts – Pie charts show your data in proportions of a whole. The total of your numbers should be 100%. Doughnut charts are included. Donut charts are good when there are multiple series that relate to a larger sum.

Bar charts – Bar charts allow you to visually compare values across a few categories when the chart shows duration or the category text is long.

Area charts – Area charts show trends over time or categories. Use it to highlight the magnitude of change over time.

Area charts – Area charts show trends over time or categories. Use it to highlight the magnitude of change over time.

Scatter charts – Scatter or bubble charts show the relationship between sets of values.

Stock, Surface or Radar charts – This category includes a number of chart types to help you show the trend of a stock's performance over time, show trends in values in a curve or with color, or show values relative to a center point.

Combo chart – Combo charts highlight different types of information when your values vary widely or you have mixed types of data.

To insert a chart, use the following procedure.

Step 1: Select the cells, including the labels to include in the chart.

Step 2: Select the Insert tab from the Ribbon.

Step 3: Select the type of chart you would like to use.

Excel displays the chart.

Overview of the Chart Tools Tabs

The Tools tabs for working with charts.

Understanding Chart Elements

The parts of a standard chart are.

- The Chart area includes all other parts of the chart that appear inside the chart window.
- A data point represents a single value in the worksheet. Depending on the type of chart, this may be a bar, a pie slice, or another shape or pattern.
- A group of related data points make up the data series. Charts usually have more than one data series, except pie charts, which only represents one data series.
- An axis is a reference line for plotting data. A two-dimensional chart has an X-axis and a y-axis. For many charts, the label is on the X-axis and the values are on the y-axis. Three dimensional charts also have a Z-axis. A pie chart does not have an axis of any type.
- A tick mark intersects an axis as a small line. It may have a label and can indicate a category, scale, or chart data series.
- The Plot area includes all axes and data point markers.
- Gridlines can make it easier to view data values by extending tick marks across the whole plot area.
- You can add text to include a label or title. The text can be attached to the chart or axis, which cannot be moved independently of the chart. Unattached text is a text box simply shown with the chart.
- The legend defines the patterns, colors, or symbols used in the data markers.

Resizing and Moving the Chart

To resize a chart, use the following procedure.

Step 1: Click on the chart to select it. Notice the border around the chart.

Step 2: Select one of the corners and drag the chart. Notice the cursor changes to a diagonal line with arrows at both ends. You can make it smaller or bigger, depending on which direction you drag.

Step 3: Release the mouse when the chart is the desired size.

To move the chart to a new worksheet in the workbook, use the following procedure.

Step 1: Select the chart.

Step 2: Select the Chart Tools Design tab.

Step 3: Select the Move Chart tool.

Excel displays the Move Chart dialog box.

Step 4: Select New Sheet.

Step 5: Give the new worksheet a new name, if desired.

Step 6: Select OK.

Excel creates a new worksheet in the workbook (notice the tabs at the bottom). The chart has also been resized to fill the worksheet.

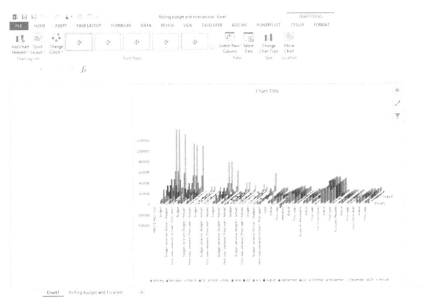

Chapter 14 – Working with Charts

Now that you have decided what type of chart to use, it is time to make your data shine. Those little icons to the right of your chart are new to Excel 2013 and will help you add chart elements, change the style and color scheme, and use data filters. You will also learn about adding and working with data labels.

Using Chart Elements

To add a chart element, use the following procedure.

Step 1: Select the + sign on the right side of your chart.

Step 2: Check the box of the element you want to add. (Or clear the box for the element you want to remove). Many of the elements include a small arrow to the right of the option. Click the arrow to see additional options.

You can also use the Add Chart Element tool from the Chart Tools Design tab on the Ribbon. Pause your pointer over an option to see a preview.

To access the additional formatting options for one or more elements, use the following procedure.

Step 1: Select More Options from either Chart Elements list (from the icon next to the chart or the Ribbon).

Step 2: The **Format** pane opens for the selected element.

Select each of the icons to see the different options, such as Fill and Line; Shadow, Glow Soft Edges and 3-D Format; Alignment; Text Fill and Outline, and more, depending on which element you selected. You can then view the options for other elements.

Using Chart Styles and Colors

To select a new chart style, use the following procedure.

Step 1: Select the chart you want to format.

Step 2: Select the paintbrush icon to the right of your chart.

Step 3: Select the desired chart style.

To select new chart colors, use the following procedure.

Step 1: Select the chart you want to format.

Step 2: Select the paintbrush icon to the right of your chart.

Step 3: Select the Color tab.

Step 4: Select the desired color palate.

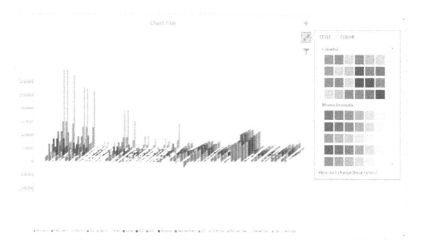

Using Chart Filters

Step 1: Select the funnel sign on the right side of your chart.

Step 2: Check the box of the value you want to add. (Or clear the box for the value you want to remove).

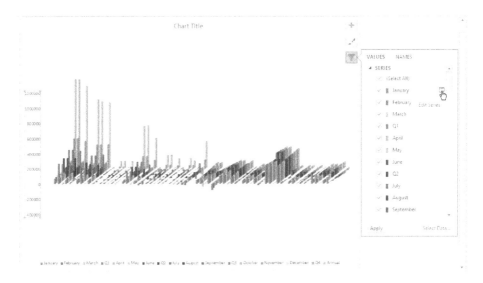

Step 3: To edit a Series name, select the worksheet icon next to the series.

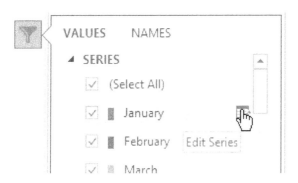

Step 4: In the **Edit Series** dialog box, enter the name you want to use.

Step 5: Select OK.

Edit Series   ?   x

Series name:
='Rolling Budget and Forecast'!$ = January
Series values:
='Rolling Budget and Forecast'!$ = , , $65,000 , ...

OK   Cancel

Working with Data Labels

To add data labels to a chart, use the following procedure.

Step 1: Select the chart that you want to label. Select the data series (such as one group of columns) or an individual data point to label, if desired.

Step 2: Select the + sign to the right of the chart.

Step 3: Check the Data Labels box and select an option from the list to the right, if desired. The options are different, based on which type of chart you have or which type of data point or series you selected.

To format data labels, use the following procedure.

Step 1: Select the chart that you want to label. Select the data series (such as one group of columns) or an individual data point to label, if desired.

Step 2: Select the + sign to the right of the chart.

Step 3: Select the small arrow to the right of Data Labels.

Step 4: Select More Options.

Step 5: In the Format Data Labels pane, you can set the Fill, Border, Effects, Size & Properties, Label Options, Text Fill, Text Effects, and Text Box options. Review each of these views of the Format Data Labels pane. Note that each set of options can be expanded or condensed using the small arrow to the left of the title.

Format Data Labels ▾ ✕

LABEL OPTIONS ▾   TEXT OPTIONS

▷ SIZE

◢ ALIGNMENT

Vertical alignment   Middle Ce... ▾

Text direction   Horizontal ▾

Custom angle

☑ Resize shape to fit text

☒ Allow text to overflow shape

Left margin   0.04'

Right margin   0.04'

Top margin   0.02'

Bottom margin   0.02'

☑ Wrap text in shape

Columns...

Format Data Labels ▾ ✕

LABEL OPTIONS ▾   TEXT OPTIONS

◢ LABEL OPTIONS

Label Contains

☐ Value From Cells

☐ Series Name

☐ Category Name

☑ Value

☑ Show Leader Lines

☐ Legend key

Separator

Reset Label Text

▷ NUMBER

Format Data Labels ▾ ✕

LABEL OPTIONS ▾   TEXT OPTIONS

▷ TEXT FILL

◢ TEXT OUTLINE

● No line

○ Solid line

○ Gradient line

Format Data Labels ▾ ✕

LABEL OPTIONS ▾   TEXT OPTIONS

◢ SHADOW

Presets

Color

Transparency |

Size |

Blur |

Angle |

Distance |

▷ REFLECTION

▷ GLOW

▷ SOFT EDGES

▷ 3-D FORMAT

▷ 3-D ROTATION

125

Format Data Labels

LABEL OPTIONS ▼ **TEXT OPTIONS**

▲ TEXT BOX

Vertical alignment	Middle Ce... ▼
Text direction	Horizontal ▼
Custom angle	

☑ Resize shape to fit text

■ Allow text to overflow shape

Left margin	0.04"
Right margin	0.04"
Top margin	0.02"
Bottom margin	0.02"

☑ Wrap text in shape

Columns...

Chapter 15 – Creating Pivot Tables and Pivot Charts

PivotTables allow you to analyze numeric data in depth. You can use this tool to answer unanticipated questions about data. PivotTables are interactive, cross-tabulated Excel reports that summarize and analyze data. In this chapter, you will learn how to insert a Pivot Table using Excel Recommendations. You will also learn how to choose fields and group data to create different types of Pivot Tables. You will gain an understanding of the PivotTable Tools tab. You will also learn how to change the data displayed and refresh the table. You will also learn how to create a PivotChart, both from an existing PivotTable and straight from data. Finally, we will look at some real-life examples of using PivotTables and PivotCharts.

Inserting a PivotTable using Excel Recommendations

To insert a PivotTable from recommendations, use the following procedure.

Step 1: Highlight the data you want to analyze.

Step 2: Select the Insert tab from the Ribbon.

Step 3: Select Recommended PivotTables.

Excel displays the Recommended PivotTables dialog box.

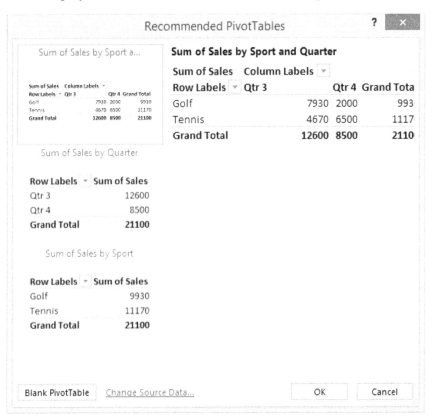

Step 4: Select the Pivot Table you want to use from the choices on the left side of the dialog box. You can see a preview on the right.

Step 5: Select OK.

Excel displays your PivotTable on a new worksheet.

Choosing Fields and Grouping Data

To add (or remove) fields to/from the PivotTable report, use the following procedure.

Step 1: Check the box next to a field listed in the PivotTable Fields pane to include it in the report. Clear a box to remove it. The default location where fields are added are as follows:

- Nonnumeric fields are added to the Row Labels.

- Numerical fields are added to the Values area.

- Date and time values are added to the Column Labels.

You can also apply a filter or sorting to one or more fields, by selecting the small arrow to the far right of the field name.

The bottom of the PivotTable Field List pane includes four areas:

- Filters

- Rows

- Columns

- Values

To group the data, use the following procedure.

Step 1: Right click on a field label in the PivotTable Field List and select one of the options from the context menu.

Step 2: You can also simply drag the fields from one area to another. You can even drag a field from the top portion of the pane to one of the bottom areas.

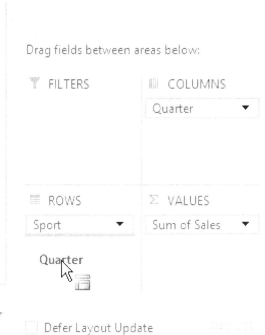

Overview of the Pivot Table Tools Tabs

The Tools tabs for working with PivotTables.

Changing the Data Displayed and Refreshing the PivotTable

To refresh the PivotTable after making a change to the data, use the following procedure.

Step 1: Return to the worksheet containing the PivotTable.

Step 2: Click somewhere on the PivotTable.

Step 3: Select the Options tab from the Ribbon.

Step 4: Select Refresh.

To change the data source, use the following procedure.

Step 1: Select the PivotTable Tools Analyze tab from the Ribbon.

Step 2: Select Change Data Source.

Excel returns to the worksheet of the source data and highlights the current data source. It also displays the **Change PivotTable Data Source** dialog box.

Step 3: Highlight the new data area on the worksheet.

Change PivotTable Data Source

Choose the data that you want to analyze

● Select a table or range

Table/Range: Sheet1!$A$1:$C$8

Use an external data source

Choose Connection...

Connection name:

OK   Cancel

Step 4: Select OK.

Step 5: Excel opens the new PivotTable. Select and group the fields as desired.

Creating a Pivot Chart from a Pivot Table or Data

To add a PivotChart from a PivotTable, use the following procedure.

Step 1: Click anywhere in the PivotTable for which you want to add a chart.

Step 2: Select the PivotTable Tools Analyze tab from the Ribbon.

Step 3: Select PivotChart.

Excel displays the **Insert Chart** dialog box.

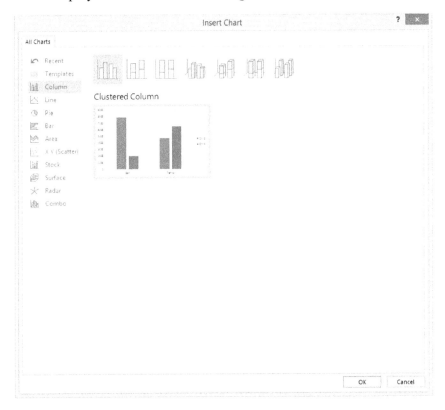

Step 4: Select the desired type of chart and select OK.

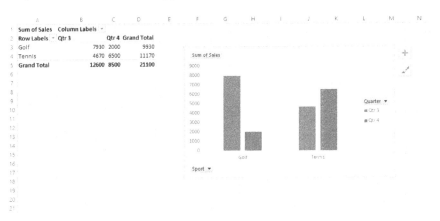

To insert a PivotChart from data, use the following procedure.

Step 1: Place your cursor somewhere in the data you want to analyze.

Step 2: Select the Insert tab from the Ribbon.

Step 3: Select PivotChart.

Excel displays the Create PivotChart dialog box.

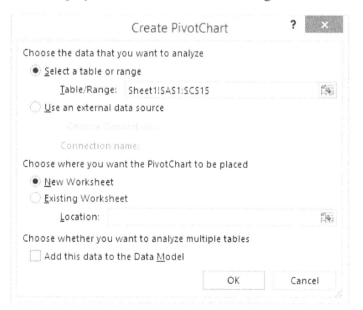

Step 4: Excel automatically provides a range of cells based on your selection. You can change the table or range if desired.

Step 5: Select a location for the PivotChart. You can have Excel create a new worksheet or select one of the existing sheets.

Step 6: Select OK.

Excel displays the blank PivotChart and the Fields pane for you to begin choosing your fields and grouping data.

Step 7: Add fields to view the chart.

Some Real-life Examples

Find out the sum of payments from each client.

Find out the sum of payments by month.

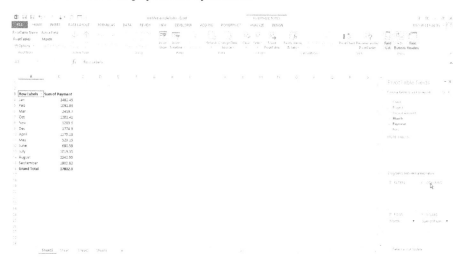

If you create a PivotTable that includes the Salesperson and the Order Amount, you get this.

Who are the top ten salesmen?

Click the arrow next to Row labels and select More Sort Options.

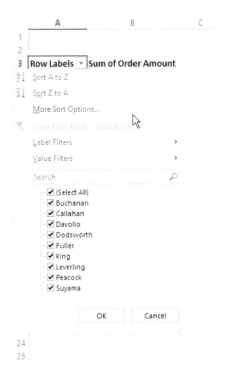

In the Sort dialog box, select Ascending (A to Z) by Sum of Order Amount and select OK.

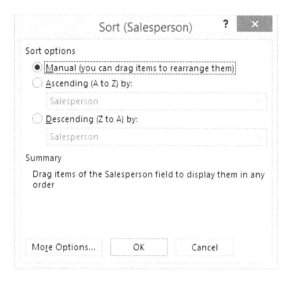

Chapter 16 – Macros

A macro is a set of recorded computer instructions. These instructions are associated with a shortcut key or macro name that makes it easy to tell your computer to run that set of instructions. This chapter will explain how to save time with macros. You will learn how to display the Developer tab, which contains the tools you will need to record macros. You will learn how to record and run macros. This chapter also explains macro security levels to avoid allowing malicious content to damage your computer with macros. Finally, you will learn how to customize and change the Quick Access Toolbar so that you have instant access to your favorite macros.

Displaying the Developer Tab

To display the Develop tab, use the following procedure.

Step 1: Select the File tab from the Ribbon.

Step 2: Select Options.

Step 3: Select Customize the Ribbon.

Step 4: In the Customize the Ribbon list on the right, check the Developer box.

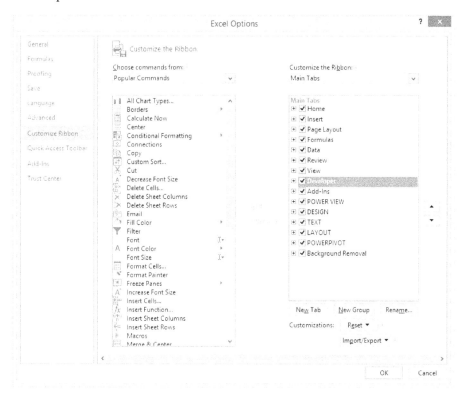

Step 5: Select OK.

The Developer tab.

Recording and Running Macros

To record a macro, use the following procedure. In this example, we will sum the column and add formatting to the numbers.

Step 1: Select the Developer tab from the Ribbon.

Step 2: Select Use Relative References.

Step 3: Select Record Macro.

Step 4: In the **Record Macro** dialog box, give your macro a name.

Step 5: To make the macro available to other worksheets, select Personal Macro Workbook from the Store Macro In drop down list.

Step 6: Select OK to begin recording.

Step 7: Perform the actions you want to record. In this example, we inserted a Sum and then formatted the total with a currency formatting and added bold face formatting.

Step 8: Select the Developer tab.

Step 9: Select Stop Recording.

To run a macro, use the following example.

Step 1: Place your cursor in the cell where you want to perform the macro.

Step 2: Select the Developer tab.

Step 3: Select Macros.

Step 4: In the **Macro** dialog box, select your macro name from the list.

Step 5: Select Run.

Note that when you close Excel, you will get the following warning message.

Select Save to keep the macro and make it available to other workbooks.

To change the macro security, use the following procedure.

Step 1: Select the Developer tab.

Step 2: Select Macro Security.

Step 3: Select one of the following options:

Disable all macros without notification – this option only runs macros in documents in trusted locations.

Disable all macros with notification – this option disables macros that are not in trusted locations, but it provides notification, so that you can choose to enable those macros on a case by case basis.

Disable all macros except digitally signed macros – this option allows not only macros in trusted locations, but also macros that are digitally signed by a trusted publisher. Other macros are disabled with notification to allow you to choose to enable those macros on a case by case basis.

Enable all macros – this option allows all macros to run, which is potentially dangerous since virus authors often use macros to distribute malicious code on computers. Microsoft does not advise using this setting.

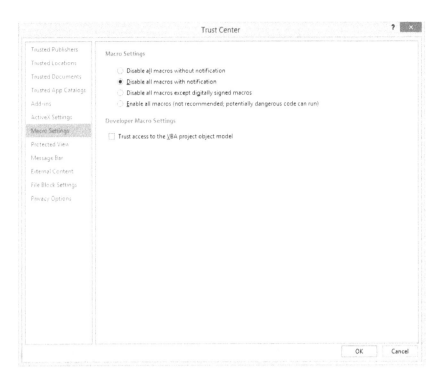

Step 4: Check the Trust Access to the VBA Project Object Model box only if you are a developer. This security option makes it more difficult for unauthorized programs to build code that self-replicates.

Step 5: Select OK.

Customizing and Changing the Quick Access Toolbar

To add a macro to the Quick Access Toolbar, use the following procedure.

Step 1: Select the arrow to the right of the Quick Access Toolbar.

Step 2: Select More Commands.

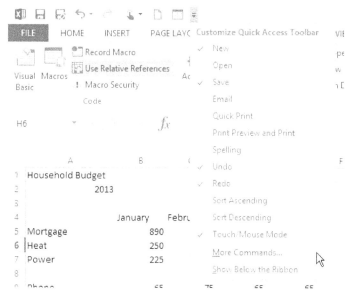

Step 3: In the Choose Command From drop down list, select Macros.

Step 4: The macro you recorded should be listed. Select it and select Add.

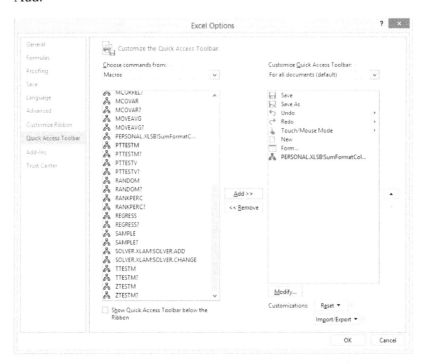

Step 5: If you would like to modify the name of the macro, select Modify.

Step 6: In the **Modify Button** dialog box, you can choose an icon to show in the Quick Access Toolbar. You can also modify the name.

Step 7: Select OK.

Step 8: Select OK in the **Excel Options** window.

Chapter 17 – Solving Formula Errors

Formula errors can be very frustrating. This chapter will teach you how to prevent formula errors by using named ranges. You will gain an understanding of formula errors and learn how to use error checking. You will also learn how to use the Trace Errors commands. Finally, we will look at how to evaluate formulas.

Using Named Ranges

To name a range, use the following procedure.

Step 1: Highlight the cell references you want to name.

Step 2: Select the Formulas tab.

Step 3: Select Define Name.

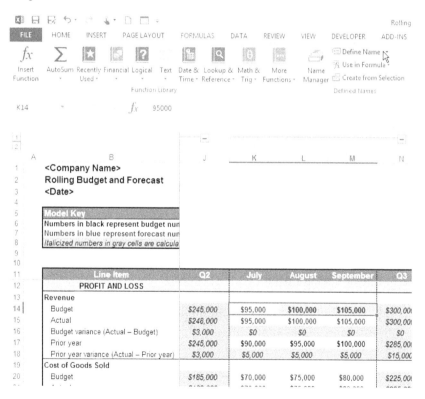

Step 4: Enter a name for the cell reference range.

Step 5: Select a different scope for the reference, if desired, from the Scope drop down list.

Step 6: Enter a Comment, if desired,

Step 7: Change the Refers to area, if desired.

Step 8: Select OK.

To use a named range in a formula, use the following procedure.

Step 1: Begin entering your formula.

Step 2: When you are ready to enter the range, select the Formula tab.

Step 3: Select Use in Formula.

Step 4: Select the named range from the list.

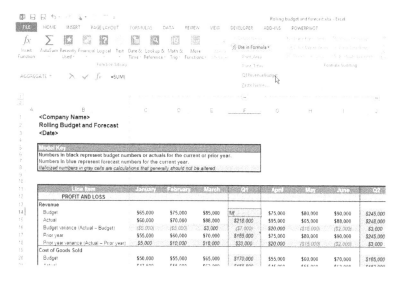

Understanding Formula Errors

Discuss the most common formula errors and how they occur.

Start every function with the equal sign (=)

Excel will display the formula contents as text or a date if you do not use the equal sign.

Match all open and close parentheses

Every parenthesis needs a pair. Parenthesis must be in the correct position for the formula to work correctly.

Use a colon to indicate a range

When working with a range of cells, you must use a colon between the first and last cell reference.

Enter all required arguments

Some functions require arguments and some do not. If the function requires arguments, make sure you have the right number.

Enter the correct type of arguments

For functions that require arguments, make sure you have the right ones.

Use the * symbol when multiplying numbers

The * symbol (asterisk) is the multiplication operator in Excel, not "x."

Use quotation marks around text in formulas

If you create a formula that includes text, enclose the text in quotation marks.

Nest no more than 64 functions

The top limit of nested functions, or functions within a function, is 64.

Enclose other sheet names in single quotation marks

If your worksheet names contain non-alphabetical characters, you must enclose the sheet name within single quotation marks when using the name in a formula.

Place an exclamation point (!) after a worksheet name when you refer to it in a formula

If you are using a worksheet name in a formula, the name must be followed by an exclamation point.

Include the path to external workbooks

If you are referencing cells from another workbook, make sure the formula includes both the workbook name and the path to the workbook.

Enter numbers without formatting

Excel treats commas as separator characters. Format the formula result after you enter the numbers in the formula.

Avoid dividing by zero

If you divide a cell by another that is zero or no value can result in a #DIV/0! Error.

Using Error Checking

The **Error Checking** dialog box, use the following procedure.

Step 1: From anywhere on the worksheet, select the Formulas tab.

Step 2: Select Error Checking.

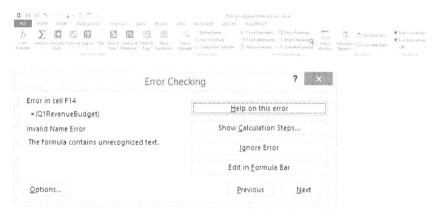

The Error Checking dialog box displays the formula as written in the cells. It explains why the formula contains an error.

- **Help on this Error** – opens the Excel help files directly to an article related to the type of error Excel detected.

- **Show Calculation steps** – opens the Evaluate Formula dialog box (discussed later in this chapter).

- **Ignore Error** – allows you to keep the error and removes the green triangle from the cell.

- **Edit in Formula Bar** – moves your cursor to the Formula bar to allow you to correct the formula.

- **Options** – opens the Options window to allow you to adjust the error checking options.

- **Resume** – restarts the Error Checking if you have switched to another task.

- **Previous** – returns to the previous error.

- **Next** – moves to the next error.

The Excel Options dialog box for Formulas.

You can open the Formulas options from the Error Checking dialog box or the Trace Errors commands next to an error cell.

You can also open the Options dialog box selecting the File tab from the Ribbon. Then select Options. Select Formulas.

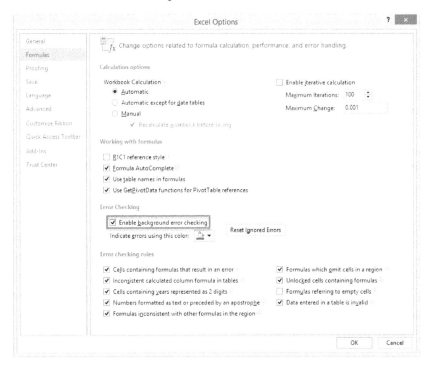

Under Error Checking, you can turn on Background error checking by checking the box.

You can change the color of the triangle displayed in cells where Excel has detected a formula error.

Select the Reset Ignored Errors to re-enable Excel to help you with any errors that you have previously ignored.

In the Error Checking Rules area, you can check or clear the following checkboxes:

- **Cells containing Formulas that result in an error** – When checked, Excel checks for formulas that do not use expected syntax, arguments, or data types.

- **Inconsistent calculated column formula in tables** – When checked, Excel checks for inconsistencies in calculated columns, such as when you enter data other than a formula in a column that has all calculated cells.

- **Cells containing years represented in 2 digits** – When checked, Excel will create an error if you enter a date with a year represented as two digits.

- **Numbers formatted in text or preceded by an apostrophe** – When checked, Excel will create an error if you enter or import numbers preceded by an apostrophe or text.

- **Formulas inconsistent with other formulas in the region** – When checked, Excel looks for formulas that are different from formulas near it. Often these formulas should be the same, except for the cell references used.

- **Formulas which omit cells in a region** – When checked, Excel compares the reference in a formula against the actual range of cells adjacent to it.

- **Unlocked cells containing formulas** – Formulas are locked for protection by default and must be unlocked before editing. If you have unlocked cells with formulas, Excel marks it as an error when this box is checked.

- **Formulas referring to empty cells** – When checked, Excel creates an error if a formula includes a reference to an empty cell.

- **Data entered in a table is invalid** – When checked, Excel creates an error if there is a validation error in a table.

Using the Trace Errors Commands

The Trace Errors Commands on a cell with a formula error, use the following procedure.

Step 1: A formula with an error displays a green triangle in the upper left corner, along with an error icon next to the cell. Click on the arrow next to the icon to see the options.

ary	February	March		Q1		April
)0	$75,000	$85,0(!	#NAME?			$75,000
)0	Invalid Name Error					$95,000
)0)						$20,000
)0	Help on this error					$75,000
0	Show Calculation Steps...					$20,000
	Ignore Error					
)0	Edit in Formula Bar		$170,000			$55,000
)0	Error Checking Options...		$165,500			$45,000
0			$4,500			$10,000
)0	$48 000	$54 000	$147 000			$49 000

- **Help on this Error** – opens the Excel help files directly to an article related to the type of error Excel detected.

- **Show Calculation steps** – opens the Evaluate Formula dialog box (discussed later in this chapter).

- **Ignore Error** – allows you to keep the error and removes the error icon and green triangle.

- **Edit in Formula Bar** – moves your cursor to the Formula bar to allow you to correct the formula.

- **Error Checking Options** – opens the Options window to allow you to adjust the error checking options (discussed later in this chapter).

Evaluating Formulas

To evaluate a formula, use the following procedure.

158

Step 1: Select the cell that contains the formula you want to evaluate.

Step 2: Select the Formulas tab.

Step 3: Select Evaluate Formula.

Step 4: Select Evaluate to see the results of the underlined portion of the formula.

Evaluate Formula	?	×

Reference:
'Rolling Budget and F...!F14=

Evaluation:
(Q1RevenueBudget)

To show the result of the underlined expression, click Evaluate. The most recent result appears italicized.

Evaluate   Step In   Step Out   Close

Step 5: Continue selecting Evaluate to see the results of each piece of the formula.

Evaluate Formula	?	×

Reference:
'Rolling Budget and F...!F14=

Evaluation:
(#NAME?)

To show the result of the underlined expression, click Evaluate. The most recent result appears italicized.

Evaluate   Step In   Step Out   Close

- If the underlined part of the formula is a reference to another formula, select Step In to display the other formula in the Evaluation box. Select Step Out to go back to the previous cell and formula. The Step In button is not available the second time a reference appears in the formula, or if the formula refers to a cell in a separate workbook.
- To see the evaluation again, click Restart.

Step 6: Select Close when you have finished.

Evaluate each of the formulas and discuss why the results are different, even though the same formula is used for each column of cells.

Chapter 18 – Using What If Analysis

"What-if" analysis allows you to have Excel change the values in cells so that you can see how those changes affect the formulas outcomes. There are three kinds of what if analysis: goal seek, scenarios, and data tables. Goal seek allows you to find the necessary value for an unknown in a formula to obtain desired results. Scenarios allow you to view multiple different possible results for up to 32 variables. Data tables allow you to quickly calculate multiple results for one or two variables in one operation. You can view and compare the results of all the different variations together on your worksheet. This chapter introduces these tools.

Using Goal Seek

To use goal seek, use the following procedure.

Step 1: When using goal seek, one value from a formula should be left blank.

Step 2: Select the Data tab from the Ribbon.

Step 3: Select What If Analysis.

Step 4: Select Goal Seek.

Excel displays the **Goal Seek** dialog box.

Step 1: In the Set Cell field, enter or select from the worksheet the cell that contains the formula. In the sample file, select $B$4.

Step 2: In the To Value field, enter the formula result you want. For example, in the sample file, you may want the resulting payment of $900. You would enter -900 because it is a payment.

Step 3: In the By Changing Cell field, enter or select the reference for the cell that contains the value you do not know. In the sample file, this is $B$3.

Step 4: Select OK.

Excel displays the **Goal Seek Status** dialog box. Select OK to close it.

You may need to reformat the cell with the new answer to view the answer in the preferred format.

Using the Scenario Manager

To add a scenario, use the following procedure.

Step 1: Select the Data tab from the Ribbon.

Step 2: Select What If Analysis.

Step 3: Select Scenario Manager.

Step 4: In the **Scenario Manager** dialog box, select Add to create a new scenario.

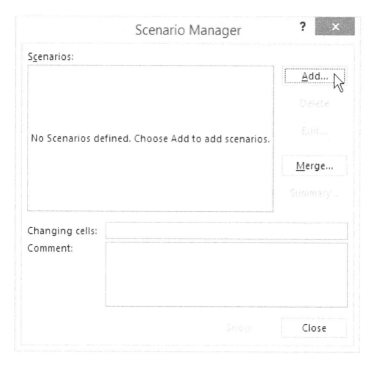

Step 5: In the **Add Scenario** dialog box, enter a Scenario Name.

Step 6: In the Changing Cells field, enter (or select from the worksheet) the multiple cells of changing values in the first scenario. Press the CTRL key while selecting each value.

Step 7: Enter a Comment, if desired.

Step 8: Protect the scenario by checking the Prevent changes and/or the Hide boxes.

Step 9: Select OK.

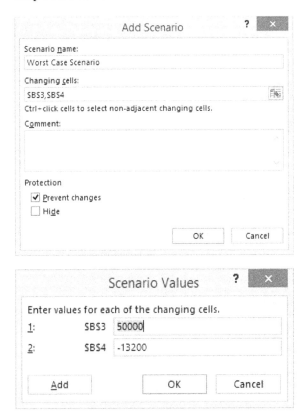

Step 10: The **Scenario values** dialog box shows the values you selected.

- For the original scenario, keep the values Excel displays.

- For each subsequent scenario, enter the new values.

Step 11: Select Add to create another set of values. If you have finished adding all the possibilities, select OK to return to the Scenario Manager.

Step 12: Repeat steps 4 through 10 to create another scenario.

Add Scenario   ?   [×]

Scenario name:

Best Case Scenario

Changing cells:

$BS3,$BS4

Ctrl-click cells to select non-adjacent changing cells.

Comment:

Protection

☑ Prevent changes

☐ Hide

OK   Cancel

Scenario Values   ?   [×]

Enter values for each of the changing cells.

1:        $B$3   150000

2:        $B$4   -2600

Add   OK   Cancel

Step 13: On the **Scenario Manager** dialog box, you can select a scenario name and select Show to see the results. The contents of the cells change, depending on which scenario you select and show. To view a report, select Summary.

Excel displays the **Scenario Summary** dialog box.

Step 14: Indicate whether Excel should display the Scenario Summary or a Scenario PivotTable Report.

Step 15: Select the cell that contains the results you want to compare (or the formula cell).

Step 16: Select OK.

Excel displays your results in the selected format.

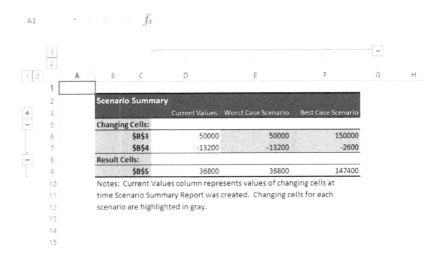

Using a One Input Data Table

To set up a one-input data table, use the following procedure.

Step 1: Enter the known values that the formula will use in evaluating the variable values.

Step 2: Enter the list of values you want to use for the input cell for the formula either down one column or across one row. If you are entering the values in a column, as shown below, leave the column to the right empty. Also leave additional rows below the values empty. If you are entering the values in a row, leave the rows below the values empty. Also leave a few columns to the right empty.

	A	B	C	D
1	Mortgage Loan Analysis			Payments
2	Down Payment	None		
3	Interest Rate		9.00%	
4	Term(months)	360	9.25%	
5	Loan Amount	80000	9.50%	
6				
7				
8				
9				

Step 3: If you have entered your data in columns, enter the formula one cell above and one cell to the right of the list of data values. You can enter additional formulas in the cells to the right of this cell to evaluate how the data values affect other formulas. If you have entered your data in rows, enter the formula one column to the left of the first value and one cell below the row of values.

Step 4: Select the data table values and the formula. In this example, the range is C2:D5.

Step 5: Select the Data tab from the Ribbon.

Step 6: Select What If Analysis.

Step 7: Select Data Table.

Step 8: Select the input cell in the formula. In a one-input data table, you will only have one input. In this example, the cell B3 is the Column Input cell.

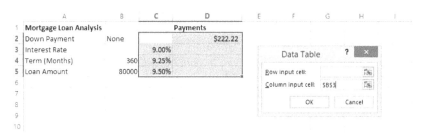

Step 9: Select OK.

For each possible value for the variable listed in the data table, Excel displays the results.

	A	B	C	D
1	Mortgage Loan Analysis		Payments	
2	Down Payment	None		$222.22
3	Interest Rate		9.00%	643.6980936
4	Term (Months)	360	9.25%	658.1403404
5	Loan Amount	80000	9.50%	672.6833657
6				

You may want to format the cells to show the results with the desired formatting (such as currency in this example).

Using a Two Input Data Table

To set up a two input data table, use the following procedure.

Step 1: Enter the known values that the formula will use in evaluating the variable values. In this example, using the previous lesson's workbook, delete the numbers except for the Loan Amount.

Step 2: Enter the formula. In this example, it should be entered in cell C2.

AGGREGATE ▾   ✕ ✓ *fx*   =PMT(B3/12,B4,-B5)

	A	B	C	D	E
1	Mortgage Loan Analysis				Payments
2	Down Payment	None	=PMT(B3/12,B4,-B5)		
3	Interest Rate		9.00%		
4	Term (Months)	360	9.25%		
5	Loan Amount	80000	9.50%		
6					
7					
8					

Step 3: Enter the list of values for the first input cell for the formula down one column under the formula. In this example, the unknown interest rate is the first input cell.

	A	B	C	D
1	**Mortgage Loan Analysis**			Payments
2	Down Payment	None	#NUM!	
3	Interest Rate		9.00%	
4	Term (Months)		9.25%	
5	Loan Amount	80000	9.50%	
6				

Step 4: Enter the list of values for the second input cell for the formula across in one row next to the formula. In this example, the unknown term is the second input cell.

Step 5: Select the range that includes data table values, the formula, and the area where Excel will display the results. In this example, the range is C2:D5.

Step 6: Select the Data tab from the Ribbon.

Step 7: Select What If Analysis.

Step 8: Select Data Table.

170

Step 9: Select the Row input cell in the formula. In this example, the cell B4 is the Row Input cell.

Step 10: Select the Column input cell in the formula. In this example, the cell B3 is the Column Input cell.

Step 11: Select OK.

For each possible value for the variable listed in the data table, Excel displays the results.

	A	B	C	D	E	F
1	Mortgage Loan Analysis		Payments			
2	Down Payment	None	#NUM!	180	240	360
3	Interest Rate		9.00%	811.41327	719.7808	643.6981
4	Term (Months)		9.25%	823.35383	732.6935	658.1403
5	Loan Amount	80000	9.50%	835.37975	745.705	672.6834

You may want to format the cells to show the results with the desired formatting (such as currency in this example).

Chapter 19 – Managing Your Data

In this chapter, you will learn how to transpose data from rows to columns. You will also learn about the Text to Columns feature. This chapter explains how to check for duplicates and create data validation rules. You will also learn how to consolidate data.

Transposing Data from Rows to Columns

To transpose data, use the following procedure.

Step 1: Copy the range of cells you want to transpose. This feature will not work if you cut the cells.

Step 2: Place your cursor in the new location and right-click.

Step 3: Select Transpose from the Paste Options on the context menu.

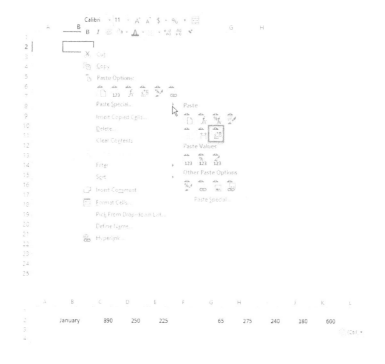

Using the Text to Columns Feature

To convert text to columns, use the following procedure.

Step 1: Paste text from another application.

Step 2: Select the text.

Step 3: Select the Data tab from the Ribbon.

Step 4: Select Text to Columns.

Step 5: In the **Convert Text to Columns Wizard**, choose the file type that best describes your data. Select Next.

Step 6: In the next screen, select the type of divider. In this example, a space separates the items we want to convert to columns. Your text could be divided by almost any character. Select Next.

Step 7: In the next screen, you see a preview of the data converted to columns. For each column:

- Define the data format (General, Text, Date) or choose to skip that column.

- Enter or select the destination on the worksheet.

Using the Advanced button, you can also choose your settings for numeric data.

Step 8: When you have finished, select Finish.

You can now work with your data as separate columns.

Checking for Duplicates

To check for duplicate data, use the following procedure.

Step 1: Highlight the area from which you want to remove duplicates.

Step 2: Select the Data tab from the Ribbon.

Step 3: Select Remove Duplicates.

Step 4: Select the columns you want to check for duplicates. The Select All and Unselect All tools can help you manage a large list of columns. The My Data has Headers box indicates whether the list includes header rows.

Step 5: Select OK.

Excel notifies you of how many duplicates are removed.

Creating Data Validation Rules

To create a data validation rule, use the following procedure.

Step 1: Select the cells where you want to apply the data validation rule.

Step 2: Select the Data tab from the Ribbon.

Step 3: Select Data Validation.

Step 4: Select Data Validation from the drop down list.

178

Step 5: On the Settings tab of the **Data Validation** dialog box, set up the Validation Criteria. Use the drop down lists to help you build your criteria. In this example, we are requiring a three-digit number.

Data Validation	?	✕

Settings | Input Message | Error Alert

Validation criteria

Allow:

Whole number ⌄   ☑ Ignore blank

Data:

between ⌄

Minimum:

100

Maximum:

199

☐ Apply these changes to all other cells with the same settings

| Clear All | | OK | Cancel |

Step 6: Select the Input Message tab.

Data Validation	?	✕

Settings | Input Message | Error Alert

☑ Show input message when cell is selected

When cell is selected, show this input message:

Title:

Account Number

Input message:

Enter a three-digit account number.

| Clear All | | OK | Cancel |

Step 7: Enter a Title and Message that the user will see when he or she selects the cell.

Step 8: Select the Error Alert tab.

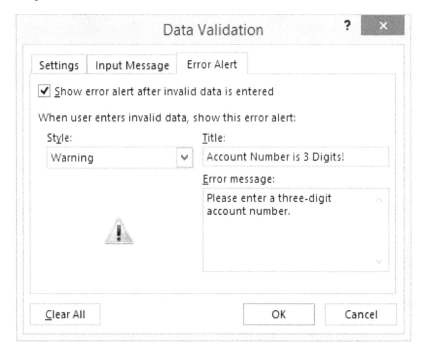

Step 9: Select the Style of error from the drop down list. Enter a Title and Error message to display if the user enters invalid data.

Step 10: Select OK.

Review what happens when you break the validation rule.

Consolidating Data

To consolidate data, use the following procedure.

Step 1: Select the starting cell where you want to display the consolidated data. Make sure to leave enough room for the consolidated data, so that you do not overwrite other information. In this example, choose the top left cell in Sheet 3.

Step 2: Select the Data tab from the Ribbon.

Step 3: Select Consolidate.

Step 4: In the **Consolidate** dialog box, do the following:

- Select the Function from the drop down list. In this example, use Average.

- Select the Reference for each worksheet you are consolidating. If the worksheet is in another workbook, select Browse to open it. Select the cells to include in the consolidation from the first worksheet and select Add. Repeat for each reference.

Chapter 20 – Grouping and Outlining Data

Excel has some powerful tools to help you quickly group and outline your data. In this chapter, you will learn how to group your data. You will also learn about adding subtotals to a list of data. This chapter explains outlining data. It also explains how to view grouped and outlined data.

Grouping Data

To create a group, use the following procedure.

Step 1: Select the range of cells you want to group.

Step 2: Select the Data tab from the Ribbon.

Step 3: Select Group.

Adding Subtotals

To add subtotals, use the following procedure.

Step 1: Make sure that each column of data has a label in the first row. It must also contain similar facts. Do not include any blank rows or columns.

Step 2: Select the Data tab from the Ribbon.

Step 3: Select Subtotal.

Step 4: In the **Subtotal** dialog box, select the locations for the subtotals from the At each change in drop down list.

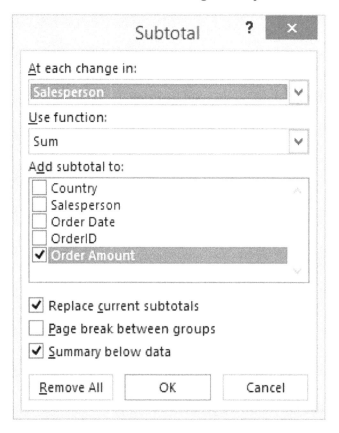

Step 5: Select the function to use in the subtotal fields from the Use Function drop down list.

Step 6: Check the boxes that correspond to your column headers for which column(s) to subtotal.

Step 7: Check the boxes to indicate the other formatting options by checking or clearing the Replace current subtotals, Page break between groups, and Summary below data.

Step 8: Select OK.

	A	B	C	D	E	F
34	UK	Buchanan	12/19/2008	10378	$103.20	
35	UK	Buchanan	12/9/2008	10372	$9,210.90	
36	UK	Buchanan	11/27/2008	10358	$429.40	
37	UK	Buchanan	11/26/2008	10359	$3,471.68	
38	UK	Buchanan	10/25/2008	10333	$877.20	
39	UK	Buchanan	10/18/2008	10320	$516.00	
40	UK	Buchanan	9/10/2008	10297	$1,420.00	
41	UK	Buchanan	8/9/2008	10269	$642.20	
42	UK	Buchanan	7/23/2008	10254	$556.62	
43	UK	Buchanan	7/16/2008	10248	$440.00	
44		**Buchanan Total**			$68,792.25	
45	USA	Callahan	5/1/2010	11056	$3,740.00	
46	USA	Callahan	4/27/2010	11034	$539.40	
47	USA	Callahan	4/24/2010	11046	$1,485.80	
48	USA	Callahan	4/22/2010	11036	$1,692.00	
49	USA	Callahan	4/21/2010	10986	$2,220.00	
50	USA	Callahan	4/17/2010	10998	$686.00	
51	USA	Callahan	4/13/2010	10997	$1,885.00	
52	USA	Callahan	4/13/2010	11007	$2,633.90	
53	USA	Callahan	4/10/2010	10977	$2,233.00	

Outlining Data

To create an outline, use the following procedure.

Step 1: Select the range of cells to include in the outline.

Step 2: Select the Data tab from the Ribbon.

Step 3: Select the small square in the corner of the Outline group.

Step 4: In the **Settings** dialog box, check the direction of the summary rows and columns.

Step 5: Check the Automatic styles box to have Excel automatically apply styles to the outline.

Step 6: Select Create.

To work with grouped or outlined data.

The Hide Detail *icon allows you to quickly hide the detail data.*

The + icons indicate hiding detail data.

The Show Detail *icon allows you to quickly show the detail data. You can select the Show Detail icon multiple times to continue expanding the current level.*

The minus icons allow you to collapse individual groups. The plus icons allow you to expand individual groups.

The numbers in the top left corner indicate a level. Click on a number to show that level.

	A	B	C	D	E	F
1	Country	Salesperson	Order Date	OrderID	Order Amount	
44		0	Buchanan Total			
144		0	Callahan Total			
262		0	Davolio Total			
304		0	Dodsworth Total			
397		0	Fuller Total			
465		0	King Total			
591		0	Leverling Total			
743		0	Peacock Total			
809		0	Suyama Total			
810		0	Grand Total			
811						

Chapter 21 – Working with Permissions and Options

This chapter introduces you to the Information tab on the Backstage View. You will learn about marking a workbook as final, which makes the workbook read-only. You will also learn about permissions – both encrypting the workbook with a password and restricting permissions. This chapter explains how to protect both the current sheet and an entire workbook's structure. You will also learn how to add a digital signature, which is helpful if your workbook contains macros that you want to share with others. Then we will move on to exploring the Excel options dialog box, where you can set advanced options and properties. We will look at managing versions, which can help you recover unsaved work if you have Autosave turned on. Finally, we will look at saving your workbook as a template to simplify new workbook creation.

Marking a Workbook as Final

To mark a workbook as final, use the following procedure.

Step 1: Select the **File** tab from the Ribbon to open the Backstage View.

Step 2: Select **Protect Workbook**.

Step 3: Select **Mark as Final**.

Step 4: Excel displays a warning message. Select **OK** to continue.

Step 5: Excel displays an information message. Select **OK** to continue.

Notice the yellow bar at the top of the workbook to indicate that the workbook has been marked as final.

Notice that on the Info tab on the Backstage View, the Permissions area has changed.

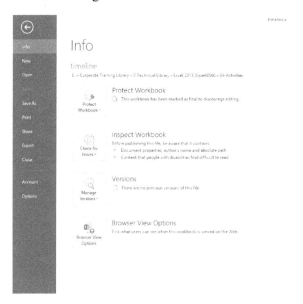

Encrypting with a Password

To encrypt a workbook with a password, use the following procedure.

Step 1: Select the **File** tab from the Ribbon to open the Backstage View.

Step 2: Select **Protect Workbook**

Step 3: Select **Encrypt with Password**.

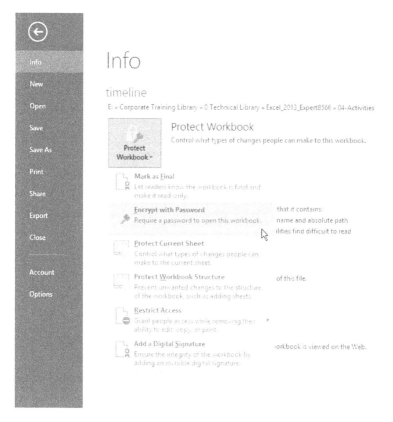

Step 4: In the Encrypt Document dialog box, enter the password that you want to use.

Step 5: In the Confirm Password dialog box, re-enter the password that you want to use to confirm it.

Note that if you want to remove the password protection, you will repeat the process. However, leave the password field blank.

Protecting the Current Sheet or the Workbook Structure

To protect a current sheet of a workbook, use the following procedure.

Step 1: Select the **File** tab from the Ribbon to open the Backstage View.

Step 2: Select **Protect Workbook**.

Step 3: Select **Protect Current Sheet**.

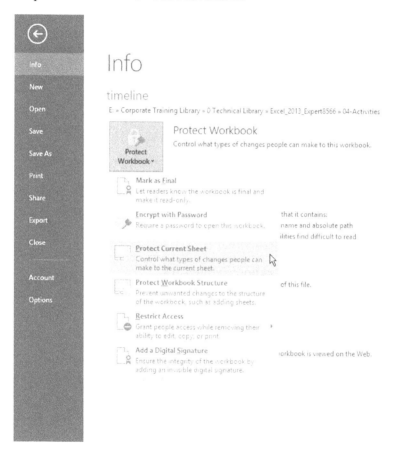

Step 4: Excel displays the Protect Sheet dialog box.

Step 5: You can enter a password if desired to unprotect the sheet.

Step 6: Check the boxes for the actions that you want to allow other users to perform on the sheet.

Step 7: Select **OK**.

To protect a workbook structure, use the following procedure.

Step 1: Select the **File** tab from the Ribbon to open the Backstage View.

Step 2: Select **Protect Workbook**.

Step 3: Select **Protect Workbook Structure**.

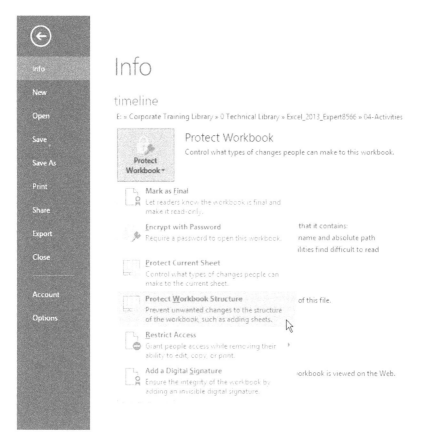

Step 4: Excel displays the Protect Structure and Windows dialog box.

Step 5: Check the boxes for the options you want to protect.

Step 6: You can enter a password if desired to unprotect the workbook.

Step 7: Select **OK**.

Adding a Digital Signature

To add a digital signature to a workbook, use the following procedure.

Step 1: Select the **File** tab from the Ribbon to open the Backstage View.

Step 2: Select **Protect Workbook**.

Step 3: Select **Add a Digital Signature**.

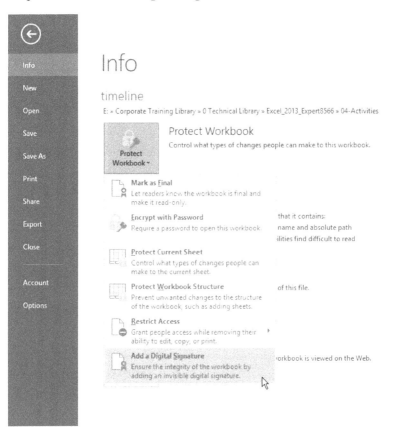

Step 4: Excel may display an informational message. Select **OK**.

Step 5: In the **Sign** dialog box, select the **Commitment Type** from the drop down list.

Step 6: Enter a **Purpose** for signing the document.

Step 7: If you would like to include additional information about the signer, select **Details**.

Step 8: In the Additional Signing Information dialog box, enter the signature information and select **OK**.

Step 9: Your **Signature Certificate** should appear in the **Signing as** area. If not, select **Change** and choose a new one from the Windows Security dialog box.

Step 10: Select **Sign**.

Step 11: The Signature Confirmation dialog box displays. Select **OK**.

Setting Excel Options

To review the options for customizing Excel, use the following procedure.

Step 1: Select the **File** tab from the Ribbon to open the Backstage view.

Step 2: Select the **Options** tab on the left.

Step 3: Here is the General tab in the Excel Options dialog box. The General tab allows you to change the user interface options. You can enter your name or initials to personalize your copy of Excel.

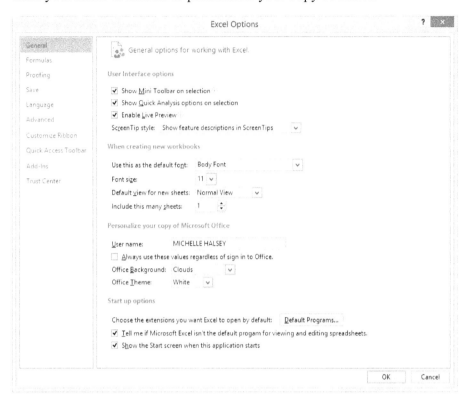

Here is the Formulas tab in the Excel Options dialog box. The Formulas tab controls your Calculation options, how you work with formulas, your error checking options, and the error checking rules.

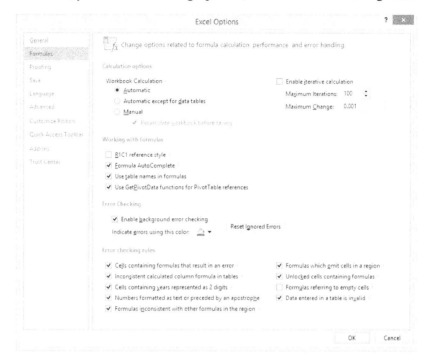

Here is the Proofing tab in the Excel Options dialog box. The Proofing tab allows you to control how Autocorrect works for spelling.

Here is the Save tab in the Excel Options dialog box. The Save tab allows you to control how workbooks are saved.

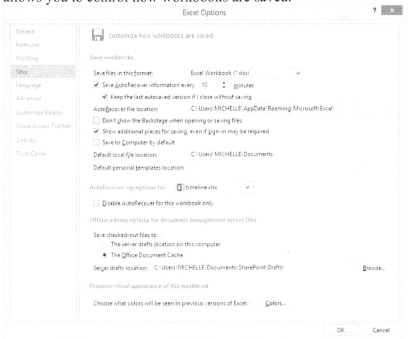

Here is the Language tab in the Excel Options dialog box. The Language tab controls your editing language and your display and help language.

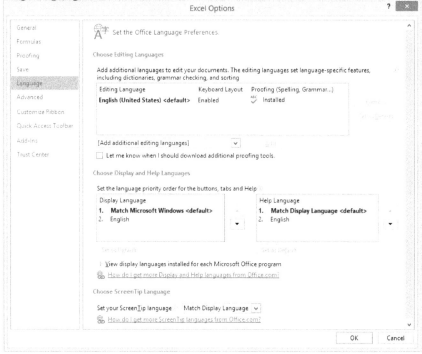

Here is the Advanced tab in the Excel Options dialog box. In the Advanced tab, you can change a number of editing options, including the default paste option and options when calculating the workbook.

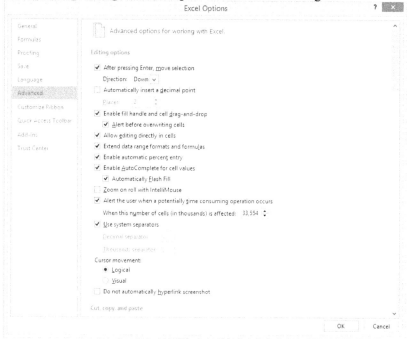

Managing Versions

To use the Manage Versions feature, use the following procedure.

Step 1: Select the **File** tab from the Ribbon to open the Backstage view.

Step 2: Select **Info**, if it is not already selected.

Step 3: The Versions area includes the most recent versions of the workbook. You can select one to return to it.

Step 4: Or, select **Manage Versions**.

Step 5: Select **Recover Unsaved Workbooks**.

Step 6: The Open dialog box displays a list of your unsaved files. Highlight the file and select **Open**.

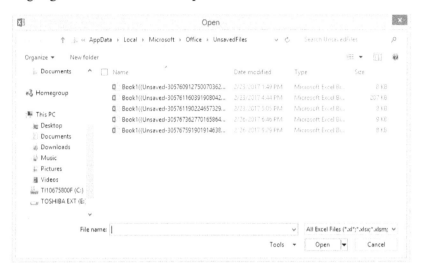

Step 7: Make sure you save the file.

Saving a Workbook as an Excel Template

To set the default template location, use the following procedure.

Step 1: Select the **File** tab from the Ribbon to open the Backstage view.

Step 2: Select the **Options** tab on the left.

Step 3: Select the **Save** tab.

Step 4: In the **Default personal templates location** field, enter the path to the templates folder you have created.

To save the current workbook as a template, use the following procedure.

Step 1: Select the **File** tab from the Ribbon to open the Backstage View.

Step 2: Select **Save As.**

Step 3: In the Save As dialog box, select **Excel Template (*xltx)** from the **Save as Type** drop down list.

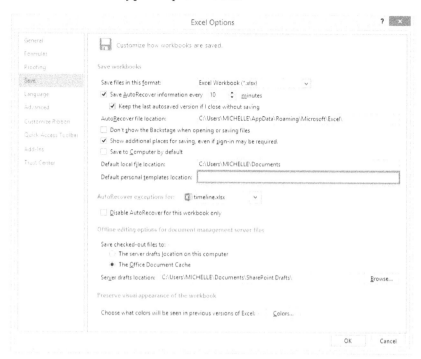

Notice that when you make that selection, the navigation changes to the default templates folder you just set. This is where you will need to save it to make it available for your use when creating new workbooks.

Step 4: Give the template a new name if desired.

Step 5: Select **Save**.

To create a new file based on the template, use the following procedure.

Step 1: Select the **File** tab to open the Backstage view.

Step 2: Select **New**

Step 3: Select **Personal**.

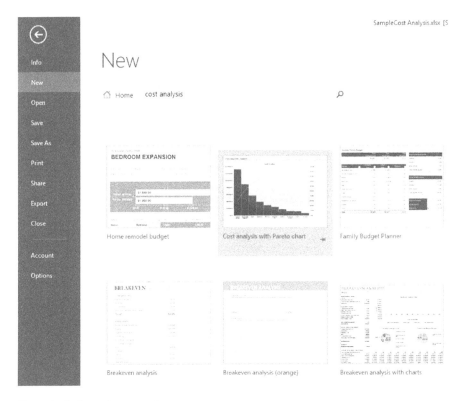

Step 4: Select the template you want to use.

Chapter 22 – Sharing Workbooks

This chapter helps you understand the issues concerned with sharing a workbook. First, we will look at how to inspect the workbook for issues. Then, you will learn how to share a workbook and edit a shared workbook. You will also learn about tracking changes to document other users changes and comments. Finally, you will learn how to merge copies of a shared workbook to consolidate the changes.

Inspecting a Document

To inspect a document, use the following procedure.

Step 1: Select the **File** tab from the Ribbon to open the Backstage View.

Step 2: Select **Check for Issues**.

Step 3: Select **Inspect Document**.

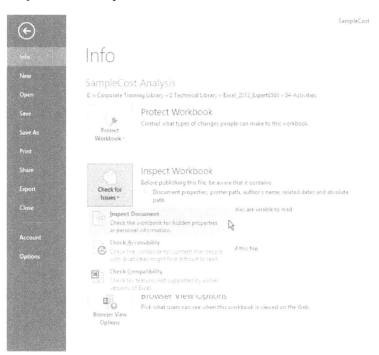

Step 4: In the Document Inspector dialog box, check the box(es) for the content you want the Inspector to find. Select **Inspect**.

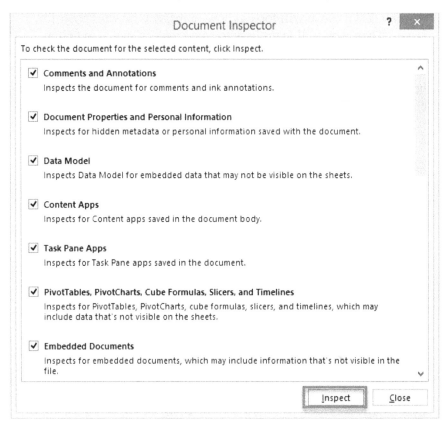

Step 5: The Document Inspector displays the inspection results.

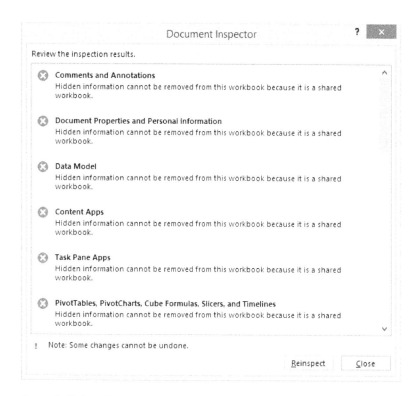

Step 6: Select **Remove All** next to an item if you want to remove it. You can also return to the workbook and make the appropriate changes.

Step 7: Select **Close** when you have finished.

Sharing a Workbook

The following features are not supported in a shared workbook. You can put these items in (and save the workbook) BEFORE you share the workbook. You will not be able to make changes to those features after the workbook is shared.

You Can Not do this in a Shared Workbook	But You Can Do This
Create an Excel table	
Insert or delete blocks of cells	Insert entire rows and columns
Delete worksheets	
Merge cells or split merged cells	
Sort or filter by formatting	Sort or filter by number, text, or date, apply built-in filters, and filter by using the Search box
Add or change conditional formats	Use existing conditional formats as cell values change
Add or change data validation	Use data validation when you type new values
Create or change charts or PivotChart reports	View existing charts and reports
Insert or change pictures or other objects	View existing pictures and objects
Insert or change hyperlinks	Use existing hyperlinks
Use drawing tools	View existing drawings and graphics
Assign, change, or remove passwords	Use existing passwords
Protect or unprotect worksheets or the workbook	Use existing protection
Create, change, or view scenarios	

Use the Text to Columns command	
Group or outline data	Use existing outlines
Insert automatic subtotals	View existing subtotals
Create data tables	View existing data tables
Create or change PivotTable reports	View existing reports
Create or apply slicers	Existing slicers in a workbook are visible after the workbook is shared, but they cannot be changed for standalone slicers or be reapplied to PivotTable data or Cube functions. Any filtering that was applied for the slicer remains intact, whether the slicer is standalone or is used by PivotTable data or Cube functions in the shared workbook.
Create or modify spark lines	Existing spark lines in a workbook are displayed after the workbook is shared, and will change to reflect updated data. However, you cannot create new spark lines, change their data source, or modify their properties.
Write, record, change, view, or assign macros	Run existing macros that do not access unavailable features. You can also record shared workbook operations into a macro stored in another nonshared workbook.
Add or change Microsoft Excel 4 dialog sheets	
Change or delete array formulas	Excel will calculate existing array formulas correctly
Work with XML data	

Use a new data form to add new data.	Use a data form to find a record.

To share a workbook, use the following procedure.

Step 1: Select the **Review** tab from the Ribbon.

Step 2: Select **Share Workbook**.

Step 3: In the Share Workbook dialog box, check the **Allow changes by more than one user at the same time** box.

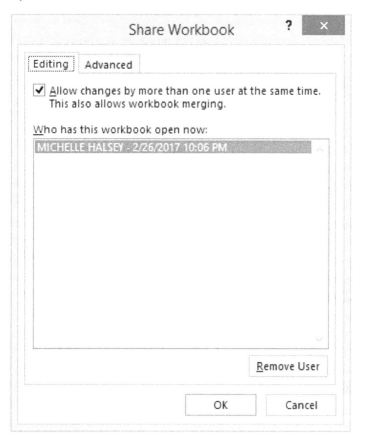

Step 4: Select **OK**.

Step 5: In the Save As dialog box, enter a new **File Name**, if desired. Navigate to the location where you want to save the workbook and select **Save**.

Note that if there are links in the workbook, you may need to verify them.

Now you can email the people who will share the workbook a link to the file or indicate the location of the file.

Editing a Shared Workbook

To edit a shared workbook, use the following procedure.

Step 1: Open the shared workbook.

Step 2: Make any necessary changes.

Step 3: Save the workbook.

You can see who else has the workbook open on the **Editing** tab of the Share Workbook dialog box.

Step 1: Select the **Review** tab from the Ribbon.

Step 2: Select **Share Workbook**.

Select the **Advanced** tab of the Share Workbook dialog box to choose to get automatic updates of the other users' changes periodically, with or without saving.

Tracking Changes

To turn on change tracking for a workbook, use the following procedure.

Step 1: Select the **Review** tab from the Ribbon.

Step 2: Select **Share Workbook**.

Step 3: Select the **Advanced** tab of the Share Workbook dialog box.

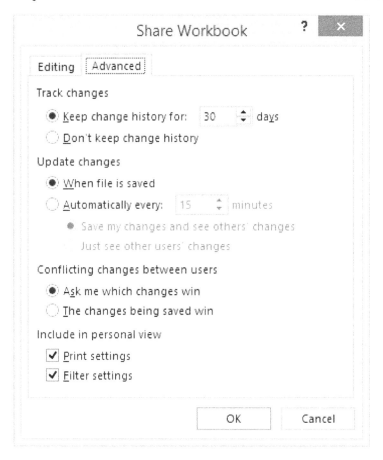

Step 4: Excel keeps the change history for a default of 30 days. You can change the number of days.

Step 5: Select **OK**.

To review the Highlight Changes dialog box, use the following procedure.

Step 1: Select the **Review** tab from the Ribbon.

Step 2: Select **Track Changes**. Select **Highlight Changes**.

Step 3: In the Highlight Changes dialog box, you can select when to highlight changes, whose changes to highlight and where to highlight the changes. Select **OK** when you have finished making your selections.

Merging Copies of a Shared Workbook

To add the Compare and Merge Workbooks command to the Quick Access toolbar, use the following procedure.

Step 1: Select the arrow next to the Quick Access Toolbar.

Step 2: Select **More Commands** from the menu.

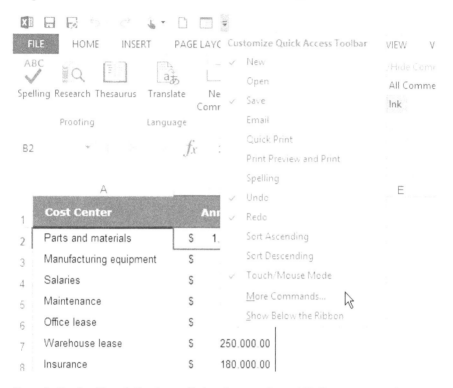

Step 3: In the Excel Options dialog box, select **All Commands** from the **Choose Commands From** drop down list.

Step 4: Highlight **Compare and Merge Workbooks** in the left list.

Step 5: Select **Add**.

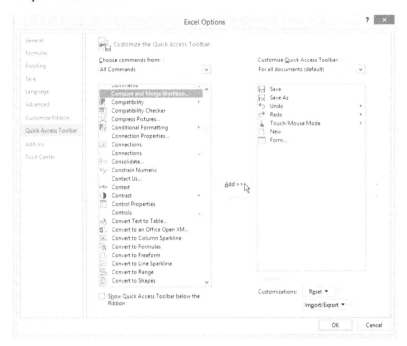

Step 6: Select **OK**.

To compare and merge workbooks, use the following procedure.

Step 1: Open the copy of the shared workbook where you want to merge the changes.

Step 2: On the **Quick Access Toolbar**, click **Compare and Merge Workbooks**.

Step 3: Save the workbook if prompted.

Step 4: In the Select Files to Merge into Current Workbook dialog box, select a copy of the workbook that contains the changes that you want to merge. Hold down CTRL or SHIFT to select multiple copies. Select **OK**.

Chapter 23 – Performing Advanced Formula and Function Tasks

This chapter will help you with formulas and calculations. We will start with learning how to use the Watch Window, where you can monitor results of different areas of your workbook and even different workbooks related to the one you are changing. Then we will learn about Excel's methodology when calculating worksheets. You will learn how to set the calculation options for the current workbook and for all workbooks. This chapter also explains how to enable or disable automatic workbook calculations. Finally, we will look at the IFERROR function, which can help you evaluate formulas and display specific results if the formula contains an error.

Using the Watch Window

To use the Watch Window, use the following procedure.

Step 1: Select the **Formulas** tab from the Ribbon.

Step 2: Select **Watch Window**.

Step 3: In the Watch Window, select **Add Watch**.

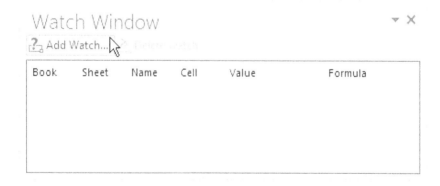

Step 4: In the Add Watch dialog box, indicate the cells that you want to watch. You can either type the cell references directly into the dialog box, or you can select the cells with your mouse.

Note that you can select more than one contiguous cell. You can even select cells on another worksheet.

Step 5: Select **Add**.

Step 6: Notice that the Watch Window has started monitoring the selected cells. It indicates the workbook and worksheet where the cell(s) reside, the name of the cell (if you named it), the cell you are monitoring, the current value, and the formula you used to create that value.

Note that you can size the window by selected Size from the arrow in the top right corner. Then drag the corners to the new size.

You can also move the Watch Window to a more convenient location on your screen. Just drag the top border to the new location. In this example, it is docked to the top of the screen, just below the Ribbon. You can also dock it to the left or the right side of the screen.

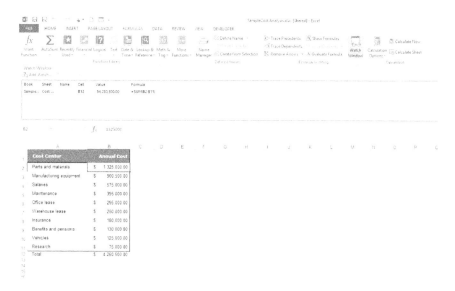

Add more areas to watch and make changes to the watched cells to see the results.

To delete a watch, highlight the item in the Watch Window you no longer need and select **Delete Watch**.

About the Excel Calculation Process

The three stages in the process of calculating data in Excel are:

- Constructing a dependency tree
- Constructing a calculation chain
- Recalculating cells

Dependency Tree and Calculation Chain

Excel uses the dependency tree to determine precedents. Excel uses this dependency tree to construct a calculation chain, which lists all cells that contain formulas in the order in which they should be calculated.

Each time the workbook is recalculated, Excel revises the Calculation chain if it comes across a formula that depends on a cell that has not been calculated. This means that calculation times improve from the first time the worksheet has been opened to the completion of the first few calculation cycles.

Dirty Cells

Anytime you make a structural change to a workbook (including entering a new formula), Excel must reconstruct the dependency tree and calculation train. Excel marks all cells that depend on a new formula or cell of data that you enter as dirty. Direct and indirect dependents are marked as dirty. At this time, Excel also detects any circular references and displays a warning message.

Excel re-evaluates the contents of each dirty cell in the order dictated by the calculation chain. With automatic calculations, the recalculation for these cells happens immediately after marking the cells as dirty.

Setting Calculation Options

Use the following procedure to set calculation options at the workbook level.

Step 1: Select the **Formulas** tab from the Ribbon.

Step 2: Select **Calculation Options**.

Step 3: Select one of the calculation options.

Step 4: If you do not use **Automatic calculation**, you can use the **Calculate Now** and **Calculate Sheet** commands in the same group on the **Formulas** tab, using the Customize the Ribbon tab on the Excel Options dialog box.

Enabling or Disabling Automatic Workbook Calculations

To use the Options dialog box to set the Calculation Options, use the following procedure.

Note that setting Calculation options in this way applies to the application level rather than the workbook level. That means it applies for all open workbooks.

Step 1: Select the **File** tab from the Ribbon.

Step 2: Select **Options**.

Step 3: Select **Formulas**.

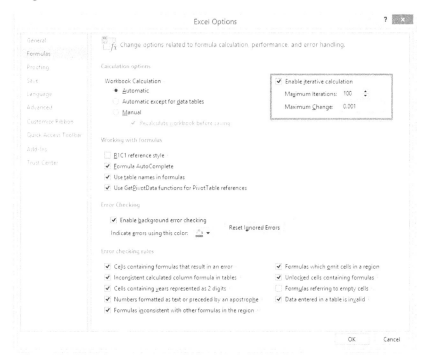

You can also set **Iterative Calculation** in the Options dialog box. Check the box and select a number of **Maximum Iterations**. Also indicate the **Maximum change** amount.

Note that the Iterative calculation options are a session-based option. That means that next time you open Excel, you will need to reset the Iterative calculation options.

Using the IFERROR Function to Evaluate Formulas

To use the IFERROR function, use the following procedure.

Step 1: In the cell that includes the formula you want to check, enter =IFERROR. When you start typing, the IFERROR function will display in a drop down menu. You can double-click to select it.

Step 2: Enter an open parenthesis, then the formula that you want to use.

Step 3: Enter a comma after the formula, then the value to display if the formula returns an error. Remember that if you want to use text, it must be in quotation marks.

Formula bar: `=IFERROR(SUMPRODUCT(C$13:S$13,C12:J12)/B12,"No Contract")`

Days	Contacts	Ex1	Ex2	Ex3	Ex4	Ex5	Ex6	Ex7	Ex8	Total
1	10	5	3	1	4	2	1	1	1	$6.50
2	8	1	5	3	0	1	2	5	5	$10.50
3	5	3	4	3	1	1	4	4	3	$17.60
4	4	4	5	3	2	1	4	5	2	$24.75
5	6	2	4	3	1	3	5	3	5	$16.67
6	5	5	4	3	1	3	3	4	3	$20.40
7	8	4	1	2	4	2	3	5	1	$10.13
8	9	2	2	5	5	4	1	3	5	$10.78
9	7	4	0	2	5	2	2	5	1	$10.71
10	0	2	1	1	0	0	0	0	0	=IFERROR(SUMPRODUCT...B12,"No Contract")
11	1	4	4	4	2	5	4	4	3	$118.00
12	10	3	1	1	1	3	3	0	3	$5.80
13	2	2	4	2	5	5	2	4	5	$53.00
14	4	5	1	3	4	0	3	2	2	$17.50
15	10	4	4	3	4	1	3	3	5	$9.60
16	10	1	3	5	5	2	2	4	4	$10.00
17	2	5	1	4	5	2	2	5	2	$47.00

Step 4: Now enter a close parenthesis and press Enter.

Step 5: Notice that when you fill the new formula into all of the cells in Column K, the division by zero errors has been replaced with the words "No Contract."

Chapter 24 – Working with Array Formulas

This chapter introduces using array formulas. We will first look at what array formulas are and some advantages, disadvantages, and rules when using them, as well as an introduction to array constants. Then you will practice creating simple and more advanced arrays.

About Array Formulas

Array formulas allow you to do complex tasks in Excel. For example, you may want to count the number of characters in a range of cells or sum only numbers that meet certain conditions. Array formulas are also known as CSE formulas because of the keystrokes you use to enter the formula (CTRL + SHIFT + ENTER).

An array is a collection of items that, in Excel, can reside in a single row, a single column or multiple rows and columns. A single-row or column array is known as a one-dimensional array (either one-dimensional horizontal or one-dimensional vertical). Multiple row and column arrays are known as two-dimensional arrays. Excel does not allow you to create three-dimensional array formulas.

An array formula can perform multiple calculations on one or more items in the array. You can return either multiple results or a single result.

Array formulas offer several advantages. They provided consistency in your workbook, which helps ensure greater accuracy. They also provide safety from accidentally overwriting a component of the array. Changes to array formulas must be confirmed by pressing CTRL + SHIFT + ENTER. Another advantage is that using array formulas result in smaller file sizes than using several intermediate formulas.

Array formulas also have some disadvantages. Array formulas are typically undocumented in a worksheet, which may cause problems if other users do not understand how to use array formulas. Also, large array formulas can slow down calculations.

Rules for entering and changing multi-cell array formulas

In addition to pressing CTRL+SHIFT+ENTER whenever you need to enter or edit an array formula, multi-cell formulas require some additional rules.

- Select the range of cells to hold your results before you enter the formula.

- You cannot change the contents of an individual cell in an array formula.

- You can move or delete an entire array formula, but you cannot move or delete part of it. In other words, to shrink an array formula, you first delete the existing formula and then start over.

- You cannot insert blank cells into or delete cells from a multi-cell array formula.

Array Constants
You use array constants as a component of array formulas. To create an array constant, you enter a list of items and surround the list with braces. For example, here is a simple array constant: ={1,2,3,4,5}

A horizontal array is created by separating the constant list items with a comma. You can create a vertical array by using semicolons instead. A two-dimensional array includes definitions for both rows and columns, so the list will use both commas and semicolons.

Constants can include numbers, text, logical values and error values. Numbers can appear in integer, decimal, and scientific formats. Remember to include text in quotation marks (""). Array constants cannot include additional arrays, formulas, or functions.

Creating One-Dimensional and Two-Dimensional Constants

To create a horizontal constant, use the following procedure.

Step 1: In the first row of the blank workbook, enter the following information:

Step 2: Select cells A1 through E1.

Step 3: In the formula bar, enter the following formula

={1,2,3,4,5}

Step 4: Press CTRL + SHIFT + ENTER.

Excel enters the constant into each cell that you selected.

To create a vertical constant, use the following procedure.

Step 1: In the first column of a blank worksheet, enter the following into cells A1 through A5:

Step 2: Select cells A1 through A5.

Step 3: In the formula bar, enter the following formula

={1;2;3;4;5}

Step 4: Press CTRL + SHIFT + ENTER.

Again, Excel enters the constant into each selected cell.

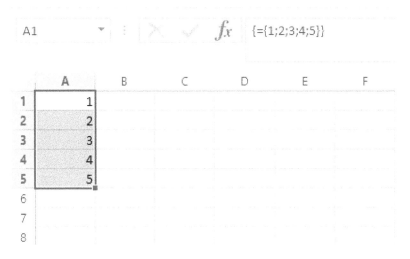

To create a two-dimensional constant, use the following procedure.

Step 1: In a blank worksheet, enter a number from 1 to 12 in each of the first four rows and first four columns, as below:

232

	A	B	C	D
1	1	2	3	4
2	5	6	7	8
3	9	10	11	12

Step 2: Select cells A1 through D3.

Step 3: In the formula bar, enter the following formula

={1,2,3,4;5,6,7,8;9,10,11,12}

Step 4: Press CTRL + SHIFT + ENTER.

Notice the results.

| A1 | | | f_x | {={1,2,3,4;5,6,7,8;9,10,11,12}} |

	A	B	C	D	E	F	G
1	1	2	3	4			
2	5	6	7	8			
3	9	10	11	12			
4							
5							
6							
7							

To use an array constant in a formula, use the following procedure.

Step 1: On the sheet from the previous procedures that includes the horizontal constant, copy the following formula in cell A3:

=SUM(A1:E1*{1,2,3,4,5})

Step 2: Press CTRL + SHIFT + ENTER.

Notice that Excel adds brackets around the entire formula. This formula multiplies the values stored in the stored array by the corresponding values in the constant. It is the equivalent of =SUM(A1*1,B1*2,C1*3,D1*4,E1*5).

To name an array constant, use the following procedure.

Step 1: Select the **Formulas** tab.

Step 2: Select **Define Name**.

Step 3: In the New Name dialog box, enter the name. In this example, we will call it Quarter1.

Step 4: In the Refers to box, enter the following constant. Remember to type the braces manually.

={"January","February","March"}

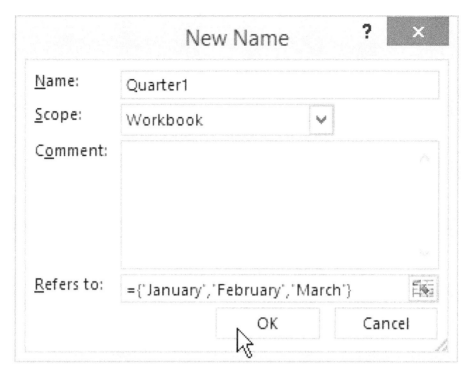

Step 5: Select **OK**.

Now let us try using the named array constant.

Step 1: Select a row of three blank cells in the worksheet.

Step 2: Enter the following formula:

=Quarter1

Step 3: Press CTRL + SHIFT + ENTER.

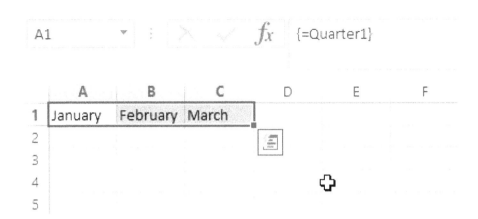

Creating a Simple Array

To create an array from existing values.

Step 1: In the sample workbook, on the Arrays worksheet, select cells C1 through E3.

Step 2: Enter the following formula in the formula bar:

=Data!E1:G3
Step 3: Press CTRL + SHIFT + ENTER.

The following result is displayed.

The formula links to the values stored in cells E1 through G3 on the Data worksheet. (You could also accomplish this by putting a separate, unique formula in each cell of the Arrays worksheet).

If you change some of the values on the Data worksheet, those changes appear on the Arrays worksheet. Remember that you will have to follow the Array rules if you need to change any of the data.

To create an array constant from existing values, use the following procedure.

Step 1: In the sample workbook, on the Arrays worksheet, select cells C1 through E3.

Step 2: Press F2 to switch to edit mode.

Step 3: Press F9 to convert the cell references to values.

Excel converts the values into an array constant.

Step 4: Press CTRL+SHIFT+ENTER to enter the array constant as an array formula.

Step 5: Excel replaces the =Data!E1:G3 array formula with the following array constant: =**{1,2,3;5,6,7;9,10,11}**

C1				f_x {={1,2,3;5,6,7;9,10,11}}		
	A	B	C	D	E	F
1			1	2	3	
2			5	6	7	
3			9	10	11	
4						
5						

This means that the link between the Data and Arrays worksheets is no longer there. The Array constant replaces the array formula.

To create an array that counts the characters in a range of cells, use the following procedure.

Step 1: On the Data worksheet, enter the following formula in cell C7:

=SUM(LEN(C1:C5))
Step 2: Press CTRL + SHIFT + ENTER.

The LEN function returns the length of each text string in the range. The SUM function then adds those values together and displays the result in the cell with the formula.

C7			f_x	{=SUM(LEN(C1:C5))}						
	A	B	C	D	E	F	G	H	I	J	K
1	400		the quick		1	2	3	4			
2	1200		brown fox		5	6	7	8			
3	3200		jumped over		9	10	11	12			
4	475		the lazy		13	14	15	16			
5	500		power user								
6	2000										
7	600		47								
8	1700										
9	800										
10	2700										
11											

To create an array that finds the N smallest values in a range, use the following procedure.

Step 1: On the Data worksheet, select cells A12 through A14 to hold the results returned by the array formula.

Step 2: Enter the following formula:

=SMALL(A1:A10,{1;2;3})
Step 3: Press CTRL + SHIFT + ENTER.

The SMALL function is evaluated three times in this formula. The result is the first, second, and third smallest members of the array contained in cells A1:A10. You could add more arguments to the constant to find more values. You could replace the SMALL function with the LARGE function to find the largest values in a range.

238

	A	B	C	D	E	F	G	H	I
1	400		the quick		1	2	3	4	
2	1200		brown fox		5	6	7	8	
3	3200		jumped over		9	10	11	12	
4	475		the lazy		13	14	15	16	
5	500		power user						
6	2000								
7	600		47						
8	1700								
9	800								
10	2700								
11									
12	400								
13	475								
14	500								
15									
16									
17									

You could also use the SUM or AVERAGE functions with this formula, such as

=SUM(SMALL(A1:A10,{1;2;3}))

=AVERAGE(SMALL(A1:A10,{1;2;3;}))

To create an array to find the longest text string in a range of cells, use the following procedure.

Step 1: On the Data worksheet, delete the contents of C7.

Step 2: Enter the following formula:

=INDEX(C1:C5,MATCH(MAX(LEN(C1:C5)),LEN(C1:C5),0),1)
Step 3: Press CTRL + SHIFT + ENTER.

Let us examine this formula, starting with the inner elements. The LEN function returns the length of each item, as shown before. The MAX function calculates the largest value among those items. Then the MATCH function calculates the offset, or relative position, of the cell that contains the longest text string. It requires three arguments, which are a lookup value, a lookup array, and a match type. The MATCH type argument is 0 in this case. Finally, the INDEX function has an array and a row and column number within that array as its arguments. The MATCH function provides the cell address.

	A	B	C	D	E	F	G	H	I	J
1	400		the quick		1	2	3	4		
2	1200		brown fox		5	6	7	8		
3	3200		jumped over		9	10	11	12		
4	475		the lazy		13	14	15	16		
5	500		power user							
6	2000									
7	600		jumped over							
8	1700									
9	800									
10	2700									
11										
12	400									
13	475									
14	500									
15										

Creating an Advanced Array

The SUM function in Excel does not work when you try to sum a range that contains an error value, such as #N/A.

To create an array that sums a range that contains error values, use the following procedure.

Step 1: In Cell K35, enter the following formula:

=SUM(IF(ISERROR(K3:K33),"",(K3:K33)))
Step 2: Press CTRL + SHIFT + ENTER.

This formula creates a new array that includes the original values, but does not include the error values.

	K35			f_x	{=SUM(IF(ISERROR(K3:K33),"",(K3:K33)))}				

	C	D	E	F	G	H	I	J	K	L	M
22	2	2	2	5	2	3	3	3	$7.70		
23	3	4	3	2	2	2	2	4	$16.40		
24	1	2	0	1	1	2	1	1	#DIV/0!		
25	3	2	4	5	4	3	2	2	$13.14		
26	4	1	4	3	5	2	5	5	$11.00		
27	3	4	5	3	2	0	5	4	$10.67		
28	3	5	3	4	5	2	1	4	$11.22		
29	2	5	4	5	5	3	5	4	$15.38		
30	3	0	5	5	1	4	2	3	$40.00		
31	4	3	5	1	1	1	0	5	$18.50		
32	2	4	2	5	5	2	4	1	$94.00		
33	1	1	4	3	3	5	4	4	$18.60		
34											
35									$672.04		
36											

To create an array that counts the number of error values in a range, use the following procedure.

Step 1: In Cell K37, enter the following formula:

=SUM(IF(ISERROR(K3:K33),1,0))
Step 2: Press CTRL + SHIFT + ENTER.

This formula is similar to the previous one, but instead of omitting the error cells from the sum, it returns the number of error values in the range.

	C	D	E	F	G	H	I	J	K	L
22	2	2	2	5	2	3	3	3	$7.70	
23	3	4	3	2	2	2	2	4	$16.40	
24	1	2	0	1	1	2	1	1	#DIV/0!	
25	3	2	4	5	4	3	2	2	$13.14	
26	4	1	4	3	5	2	5	5	$11.00	
27	3	4	5	3	2	0	5	4	$10.67	
28	3	5	3	4	5	2	1	4	$11.22	
29	2	5	4	5	5	3	5	4	$15.38	
30	3	0	5	5	1	4	2	3	$40.00	
31	4	3	5	1	1	1	0	5	$18.50	
32	2	4	2	5	5	2	4	1	$94.00	
33	1	1	4	3	3	5	4	4	$18.60	
34										
35									$672.04	
36										
37									2	
38										

In the next example, let us imagine that you need to sum just the positive integers in a range named Sales, which is already defined on Sheet 2.

To create an array that sums values based on conditions, use the following procedure.

Step 1: In cell K 39, enter the following formula:

=SUM(IF(Sales>0,Sales))
Step 2: Press CTRL + SHIFT + ENTER.

The IF function creates an array of positive values and false values. The SUM function ignores the false values.

	C	D	E	F	G	H	I	J	K	L
22	2	2	2	5	2	3	3	3	$7.70	
23	3	4	3	2	2	2	2	4	$16.40	
24	1	2	0	1	1	2	1	1	#DIV/0!	
25	3	2	4	5	4	3	2	2	$13.14	
26	4	1	4	3	5	2	5	5	$11.00	
27	3	4	5	3	2	0	5	4	$10.67	
28	3	5	3	4	5	2	1	4	$11.22	
29	2	5	4	5	5	3	5	4	$15.38	
30	3	0	5	5	1	4	2	3	$40.00	
31	4	3	5	1	1	1	0	5	$18.50	
32	2	4	2	5	5	2	4	1	$94.00	
33	1	1	4	3	3	5	4	4	$18.60	
34										
35									$672.04	
36										
37									2	
38										
39									603.6595	
40										
41										

To create an array that computes an average that excludes zeros, use the following procedure.

Step 1: In cell D35, enter the following formula:

=AVERAGE(IF((D3:D33)<>0,(D3:D33)))

Step 2: Press CTRL + SHIFT + ENTER.

243

Chapter 25 – Working with Macros

In this chapter, you will learn how to assign a macro you have created to a command button, which you can easily access each time you want to run the macro. You will also learn how to set up a graphical area that causes a macro to run when it is clicked. Similarly, this chapter explains how to run a macro automatically when a spreadsheet is opened. Finally, you will learn how to change a macro.

Assigning a Macro to a Command Button

To assign a new macro to a command key, use the following procedure.

Step 1: Select the **File** tab from the Ribbon to open the Backstage view.

Step 2: Select the **Options** tab on the left.

Step 3: Select **Customize Ribbon**.

Step 4: In the **Choose commands from** drop down list, select Macros.

You will need to create a Custom Group on the Ribbon before you can assign a macro to a Ribbon tab.

Step 1: Select **New Group.**

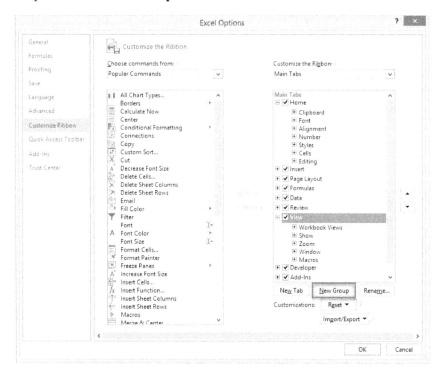

Step 2: Select **Rename**.

Step 3: Enter a new **Display name**.

Step 4: Select **OK**.

Now add the macro to the group.

Step 1: In the Customize the Ribbon list, select the ribbon where you would like to display the Macro command button.

Step 2: In the **Choose Command from** list, select your macro.

Step 3: Select **Add**.

Step 4: Select **Rename**.

Step 5: Select an icon for the macro from the list of **Symbols**.

Step 6: Select **OK**.

Now look at the selected Ribbon and see the macro command that you added.

Running a Macro by Clicking an Area of a Graphic Object

To assign a macro to a graphical object, use the following procedure.

Step 1: Insert a shape. To do this, select the **Insert** tab from the Ribbon. Select **Shapes**. Select the shape you want to insert.

Step 2: Right-click on the shape.

Step 3: Select Assign Macro from the context menu.

Step 4: Select the **Macro name** from the list. You can choose the location where the **Macro is stored by** selecting a new option from the Macros in drop down list.

Step 5: Select **OK**.

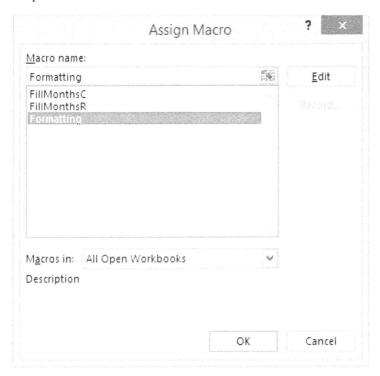

Now try running the macro by clicking on the object.

You can format the shape in any way desired.

Configuring a Macro to Run Automatically Upon Opening the Workbook

To create an Auto_Open macro, use the following procedure.

Step 1: Select the **View** tab from the Ribbon.

Step 2: Select **Macros**.

Step 3: Select **Record Macro.**

Step 4: In the **Macro name** box, enter Auto_Open as the name.

Step 5: In the **Store macro in** list, select the workbook where you want to store the macro from the drop down list.

Step 6: Select **OK**.

Step 7: Perform the actions that you want the macro to perform. For a simple example, simply select **Zoom to Selection** from the **View** tab.

Step 8: Select **Macros** from the **View** tab. Select **Stop Recording**.

Step 9: Save the workbook. You will need to select Excel macro-Enabled Workbook (*.xlsm) from the Save as type drop down list.

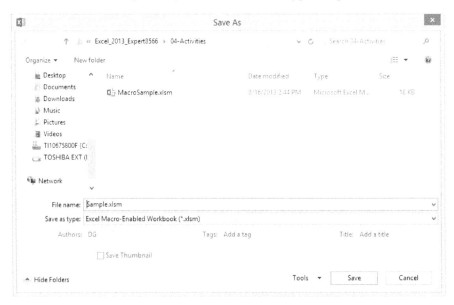

To test out your auto macro, close the workbook and reopen it. The macro is performed as soon as you open the workbook.

Recording an Auto_Open macro has the following limitations:

- If the workbook where you save the Auto_Open macro already contains a VBA procedure in its Open event, the VBA procedure for the Open event will override all actions in the Auto_Open macro.

- An Auto_Open macro is ignored when a workbook is opened programmatically by using the Open method.

- An Auto_Open macro runs before any other workbooks open. Therefore, if you record actions that you want Excel to perform on the default Book1 workbook or on a workbook that is loaded from the XLStart folder, the Auto_Open macro will fail when you restart Excel, because the macro runs before the default and startup workbooks open.

To start a workbook without running an Auto_Open macro, hold down the SHIFT key when you start Excel.

Changing a Macro

To change the name of a macro, use the following procedure.

Step 1: Select the **View** tab from the Ribbon.

Step 2: Select **Macros.**

Step 3: Select **View Macros.**

Step 4: In the Macro dialog box, select the name of the macro that you want to change. We will use FillMonths for this example.

Step 5: Select **Edit**.

The Visual Basic Editor opens with your macro. The macro is a sub-routine in the programming. We will make a copy of our FillMonths() macro, or subroutine, and change both of the new macros slightly.

```
Sub FillMonths()
'
' FillMonths Macro
'

'
    ActiveCell.Select
    ActiveCell.FormulaR1C1 = "Jan"
    ActiveCell.Select
    Selection.AutoFill Destination:=ActiveCell.Range("A1:L1"), Type:= _
        xlFillSeries
    ActiveCell.Range("A1:L1").Select
End Sub
```

First, we will make a copy of the macro.

Step 1: Select everything from Sub FillMonths() to End Sub.

Step 2: Select Copy. (CTRL + C)

Step 3: Place your cursor below End Sub.

Step 4: Paste by pressing CTRL + V.

```
Sub FillMonths()
'
' FillMonths Macro
'

'
    ActiveCell.Select
    ActiveCell.FormulaR1C1 = "Jan"
    ActiveCell.Select
    Selection.AutoFill Destination:=ActiveCell.Range("A1:L1"), Type:= _
        xlFillSeries
    ActiveCell.Range("A1:L1").Select
End Sub

Sub FillMonths()
'
' FillMonths Macro
'

'
    ActiveCell.Select
    ActiveCell.FormulaR1C1 = "Jan"
    ActiveCell.Select
    Selection.AutoFill Destination:=ActiveCell.Range("A1:L1"), Type:= _
        xlFillSeries
    ActiveCell.Range("A1:L1").Select
End Sub
|
```

Now we are going to change the name of the first macro.

Step 1: At the top of the first subroutine, enter an R next to FillMonths, to represent, fill months row. Remember that macro names cannot contain spaces.

Now we are going to change the name of the second macro. Look for the line that divides the subroutines.

Step 2: Enter a C next to FillMonths, to represent fill months column.

Now we are going to change the second macro so that it fills down instead of across and it uses the number representation of the months instead of the names.

Step 3: In the following line, change "Jan " to 1

ActiveCell.FormulaR1C1 = "Jan"
The result should be

ActiveCell.FormulaR1C1 = 1

Step 4: Now change the range so that it is a column. You will need to change "A1:L1" to "A1:A12" in two places.

Now when you return to the Macros dialog box, you see that there are two separate macros with the names we assigned. Practice running them to see how they work.

Chapter 26 – Working with Forms

This chapter takes a closer look at forms. Really, all Excel spreadsheets are a type of form where you can enter data. However, we will take a look at data forms and form controls a little more closely as other ways to collect information with more flexibility. You will also learn how to create and use a data form, including adding a new row of data, finding information by navigating or by entering search criteria, and changing or deleting a row of data. Next, we will look at some specific examples of using different types of form controls. This chapter covers the list box control, the combo box control, the spin button control, and the scroll bar control.

About Excel Forms, Form Controls, and Active X Controls

Data Forms

Data forms are a convenient way to display one complete row of information in a range or table without having to scroll horizontally. Data forms work best when you have column headings that can work as your labels and you do not need sophisticated or custom form features.

Excel can automatically generate a built-in data form for a range or table in your worksheet. The form is displayed as a dialog box, in which each label has an adjacent blank text box. There is a maximum of 32 columns you can use for one data form.

Later in the chapter, you will learn how to create a data form, update rows, and delete rows. You will also learn how to navigate using the data form and how to find a row. Data forms can display a formula result as one of the items, but formulas cannot be changed using the data form.

Worksheets with Form and ActiveX Controls
Worksheets already contain some controls as part of the basic functionality of Excel. For example, you can create labels in cells and format them. You can use comments, hyperlinks, background images, data validation and conditional formatting, as well as other features, like controls.

However, you can also add a number of other controls and customize their properties to fine-tune your worksheet. For example, you can use a list box control to make it easier to select from a list of items.

Controls are placed on the drawing canvas of the worksheet, which means that the controls and objects are independent of row and column boundaries. However, you can also set controls to move and resize with a cell.

We will take about form controls and list controls. You can also use objects drawn with Drawing tools as controls, such as AutoShapes, WordArt, SmartArt and text boxes.

Form Controls
Here is a summary of the form controls in Excel 2013:

- Label – identifies the purpose of a cell or text box, or displays descriptive information like titles, captions, pictures or brief instructions

- Group box – groups related controls into one visual unit in a rectangle with a label (optional)

- Button – runs a macro that performs an action

- Check box – turns a value on or off, and is independent of other checkboxes that may appear in the same group

- Option (radio) button – allows a single choice within a set of mutually exclusive choices usually within a group box

- List box – displays a list of one or more items available as a choice and can be controlled as a single-selection list box, a multiple selection list box (must be adjacent choices) or an extended selection list box (allows multiple noncontiguous choices)

- Combo box – combines a text box with a list box to create a drop down list box, which is like a list box, but more compact and requires the user to click the down arrow

- Scroll bar – allows the user to scroll through a range of values either by clicking the arrows or dragging the scroll bar

- Spin button – increases or decreases a value by clicking the up or down arrow

ActiveX Controls

ActiveX controls are much like form controls, except they allow more flexible design requirements, including appearance, behavior, fonts, and other characteristics. Many can be used with or without VBA code, although some can only be used with VBA UserForms. You cannot use ActiveX controls on chart sheets or XLM macro sheets. Here is a summary of the ActiveX controls in Excel 2013:

- Check box – turns a value on or off, and is independent of other checkboxes that may appear in the same group

- Text box – enables you to view type or edit text or data bound to a cell

- Button – runs a macro that performs an action. You cannot assign a macro to run directly from an ActiveX button the same way you can from a form control.

- Option (radio) button – allows a single choice within a set of mutually exclusive choices usually within a group box

- List box – displays a list of one or more items available as a choice and can be controlled as a single-selection list box, a multiple selection list box (must be adjacent choices) or an extended selection list box (allows multiple noncontiguous choices)

- Combo box – combines a text box with a list box to create a drop down list box, which is like a list box, but more compact and requires the user to click the down arrow

- Toggle button – indicates a state (like yes or no or on or off) that alternates between enabled and disabled

- Spin button – increases or decreases a value by clicking the up or down arrow

- Scroll bar – allows the user to scroll through a range of values either by clicking the arrows or dragging the scroll bar

- Label – identifies the purpose of a cell or text box, or displays descriptive information like titles, captions, pictures or brief instructions

- Image – embeds a picture file (such as bitmap, JPEG, or GIF)

- More controls – allows you to choose from additional controls

Using a Data Form

You will need to add the Form button to the Ribbon or the Quick Access Toolbar, use the following procedure to add it to the Quick Access Toolbar.

Step 1: Select the arrow by the Quick Access Toolbar.

Step 2: Select **More Commands**.

Step 3: In the Excel Options dialog box, select **All Commands** from the **Choose Commands from** list.

Step 4: Select **Form** from the list on the left.

Step 5: Select **Add**.

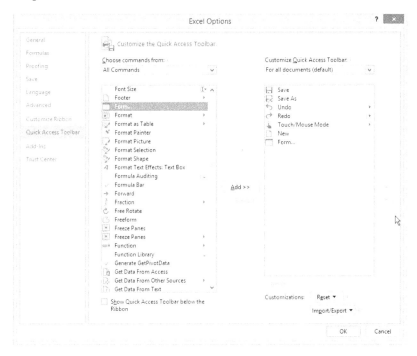

Step 6: Select **OK** to close the dialog box.

Now you can create your form, use the following procedure.

Step 7: With your cursor anywhere in the data on the worksheet, select the Form tool from the Quick Access Toolbar.

Your form is automatically created.

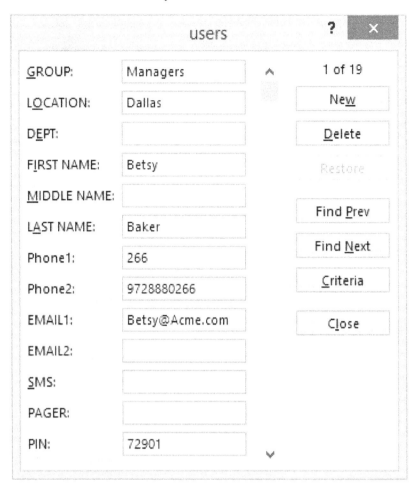

To add a new row of data, use the following procedure.

Step 1: In the data form, select **New**.

Step 2: Enter the information into each text field. You can press the TAB key to go to the next field. Press **Enter** to complete the record and go to another new record. Excel extended the worksheet behind the form down for each new record you create.

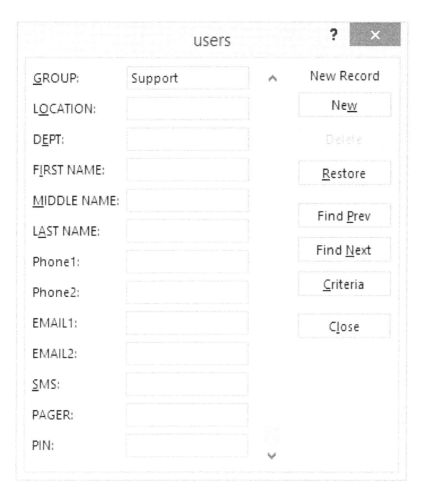

To find a row by navigating. Use the following controls:

- The scroll bar allows you to move through one row at a time. Select the up or down arrows to move through the data.

- The scroll bar also allows you to move through the data 10 rows at a time. Select the scroll bar in the area in between the arrows.

- **Find Prev** allows you to move to the previous row in the data.

- **Find Next** allows you to move to the next row in the data.

To find a row by searching, use the following procedure.

Step 1: Select **Criteria**.

Excel displays a blank form.

users	? ✕

GROUP: `Support`   ∧   New Record

LOCATION: `New York`   Ne<u>w</u>

DEPT: Delete

FIRST NAME:

MIDDLE NAME: <u>R</u>estore

LAST NAME: Find <u>P</u>rev

Phone1:   `216`   Find <u>N</u>ext

Phone2:   <u>C</u>riteria

EMAIL1:   C<u>l</u>ose

EMAIL2:

SMS:

PAGER:

PIN: `72919`   ∨

Step 2: Enter information in one or more fields to indicate your criteria. You can select **Clear** to start over. You can also use the following wildcards:

- ? to replace a single character (sm?th finds "smith" and "smyth")

- * to find any number of characters (*east finds "northeast" and "southeast")

- ~ followed by wildcard character finds a question mark, an asterisk or a tilde

Step 2: You can now scroll (**Find Prev** or **Find Next**) through any matching records.

users ? ✕

GROUP:	Support	^
LOCATION:	New York	
DEPT:		
FIRST NAME:		
MIDDLE NAME:		
LAST NAME:		
Phone1:	216	
Phone2:		
EMAIL1:		
EMAIL2:		
SMS:		
PAGER:		
PIN:	72919	v

New Record

New

Delete

Restore

Find Prev

Find Next

Criteria

Close

Step 3: Select **Form** to return to the form.

To change the data in a row, use the following procedure.

Step 1: If you have not yet entered the data by pressing **Enter**, you can select **Restore** to return the data to what is stored on the worksheet.

Step 2: Otherwise, first find the row you want to change. Then simply type over the old data.

Step 3: Press **Enter** to update the row.

To delete a row, use the following procedure.

Step 1: Find the row that you want to delete.

Step 2: Select **Delete**.

Step 3: In the confirmation message, select **OK**. Note that you cannot undo a row deletion after you have confirmed it.

Using a List Box Control

To insert a list box form control, use the following procedure.

Step 1: Make sure the **Developer** tab is showing. If not, go to **Options**, **Customize Ribbon** and check the **Developer** checkbox.

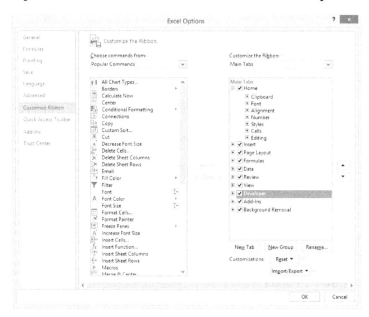

Step 2: Select the **Developer** tab on the Ribbon.

Step 3: Select **Insert**. Select **List Box Form** from the drop down list.

Step 4: Click and drag the mouse to draw the list box. In this example, start at B2 and drag down to E10.

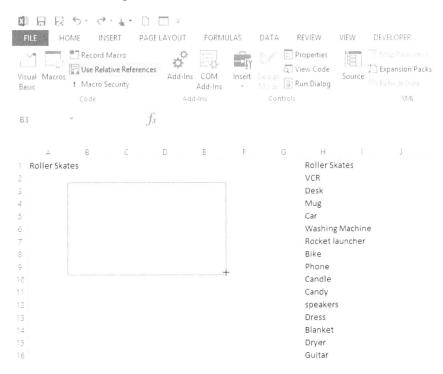

Now we need to format the list box. With the list box still selected, select **Properties** from the **Developer** tab on the Ribbon.

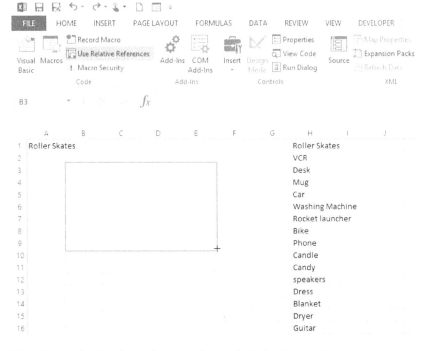

The **Control** tab of the Format Control dialog box allows you to indicate an input range and a cell link.

Step 5: In the **Input range** field, enter or select cells H1:H20.

Step 6: The **Cell link** field will put a number value in the linked cell. We will do this so our INDEX formula (which references cell G1) in cell A1 will return the list box choice. Enter or select **G1** for the **Cell link** field.

Step 7: Make sure the **Single** option is selected.

Step 8: Select **OK**.

Step 9: Now click anywhere besides the list box to deselect it. When you select an item in the list, the INDEX formula in cell A1 uses the selection to display the item's name.

Using a Combo Box Control

To insert a combo box form control, use the following procedure.

Step 1: Select the **Developer** tab.

267

Step 2: Select **Insert**. Select **Combo Box Form** from the drop down list.

Step 3: Click and drag the mouse to draw the combo box.

Step 4: Right-click the combo box, and select **Format Control** from the drop down list.

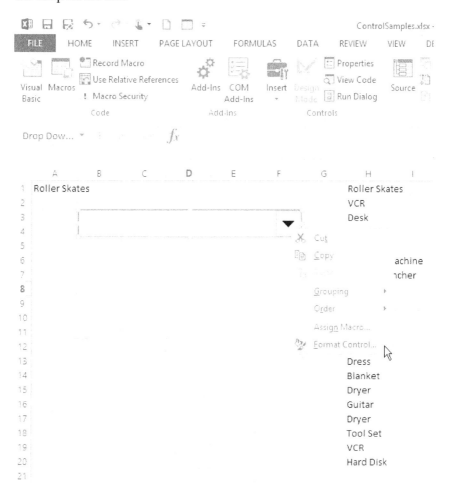

Step 5: In the **Input range** field, enter or select cells H1:H20.

Step 6: The **Cell link** field will put a number value in the linked cell. We will do this so our INDEX formula (which references cell G1) in cell A1 will return the list box choice. Enter or select **G1** for the **Cell link** field.

Step 7: The **Drop down lines** indicates the number of lines that show in the list at one time.

Step 8: Select **OK**.

Step 9: Now click anywhere besides the combo box to deselect it. When you select the arrow and choose an item from the list, the INDEX formula in cell A1 uses the selection to display the item's name.

Using a Spin Button Control

To insert a list spin button control, use the following procedure.

Step 1: Select the **Developer** tab.

Step 2: Select **Insert**. Select **Spin Button** from the drop down list.

Step 3: Click and drag the mouse to draw the spin button control.

Step 4: Right-click the spin button control, and select **Format Control** from the drop down list.

Step 5: On the **Control** tab of the Format Control dialog box, enter **1** in the **Current Value** field.

Step 6: Also enter **1** as the **Minimum Value** to restrict the top of the spin button to the first item in our list.

Step 7: Enter **20** as the **Maximum value** to specify the maximum number of entries in the list.

Step 8: Enter **1** as the **Incremental Change**.

Step 9: To put a number value in cell G1 for our INDEX formula in this example, enter **G1** in the **Cell link** field.

Step 10: Select **OK**.

Format Object

| Size | Protection | Properties | Alt Text | Control |

Current value: 1

Minimum value: 1

Maximum value: 20

Incremental change: 1

Page change:

Cell link: $G$1

☑ 3-D shading

OK   Cancel

Step 11: Now click anywhere besides the spin button to deselect it. When you click the up or down controls, cell G1 is updated. The INDEX formula in cell A1 uses the value in G1 to display the item's name.

Using a Scroll Bar Control

To insert a list scroll bar control, use the following procedure.

Step 1: Select the **Developer** tab.

Step 2: Select **Insert**. Select **Scroll Bar** from the drop down list.

Step 3: Click and drag the mouse to draw the scroll bar control.

Step 4: Right-click the scroll bar control, and select **Format Control** from the drop down list.

Step 5: On the **Control** tab of the Format Control dialog box, enter **1** in the **Current Value** field.

Step 6: Also enter **1** as the **Minimum Value** to restrict the top of the scroll bar to the first item in our list.

Step 7: Enter **20** as the **Maximum value** to specify the maximum number of entries in the list.

Step 8: Enter **1** as the **Incremental Change**.

Step 9: In the **Page Change** field, enter **5** to control how much the current value increments if you click inside the scroll bar instead of on the arrows.

Step 10: To put a number value in cell G1 for our INDEX formula in this example, enter **G1** in the **Cell link** field.

Step 11: Select **OK**.

Step 12: Now click anywhere besides the scroll bar to deselect it. When you click the up or down arrows or anywhere in the scroll bar, cell G1 is updated. The INDEX formula in cell A1 uses the value in G1 to display the item's name.

Chapter 27 – Applying Advanced Chart Features

In this chapter, you will learn about some advanced chart features. First, we will look at the different types of trend lines to help you analyze your data. You will also learn how to add a trend line. Then, we will take a look at how to plot one of your data series on a secondary axis. Finally, you will learn how to save a chart you have formatted to your liking as a chart template to be available for use when creating other new charts.

About Trend Lines

You can add one of six different trend or regression types, depending on the type of data that you have.

Note that a trend line is most accurate when its R-squared value is at or near 1. You can display the R-squared value that Excel calculates on your chart.

The following types of trend lines are available.

Linear trend line – this trend line is a best-fit straight line used with simple linear sets.

Logarithmic trend line – this trend line is a best-fit curved line used when the rate of change in the data increases or decreases quickly and then levels out. It can use either negative or positive values.

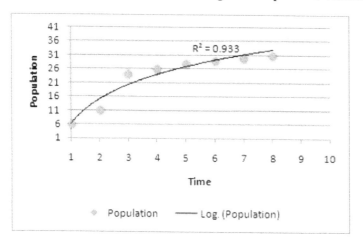

Polynomial trend line – this trend line is a curved line that is used when data fluctuates, such as to analyze gains and losses over a large data set. The polynomial order can be determined by the number of fluctuations in the data or by how many hills and valleys appear in the curve. For example, an Order 2 polynomial trend line has one hill or valley; order 3 has 2 hills or valley, and so on.

Power trend line – this trend line is a curved line that is used with data sets that compare measurements that increase at a specific rate. Data sets for this type of trend line cannot include 0 or negative values.

Exponential trend line – this trend line is a curved line that is used with data sets that rise or fall at a constantly increasing rate. Data sets for this type of trend line cannot include 0 or negative values.

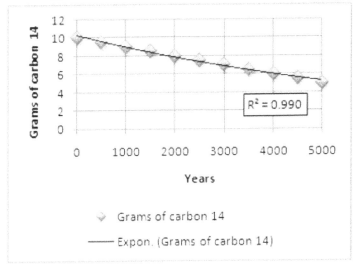

Moving Average Trend Lines – this trend line smooths fluctuations in data to show a pattern or trend more clearly. It uses a specific number of data points in an average to display the points in the line, such as 2 periods to create the first point in the trend line.

Add a Trend Line

To add a Trend Line to a chart, use the following procedure.

Step 1: Select the chart in your worksheet.

Step 2: Select the data series that you want to plot. A colored border appears around that area in the data.

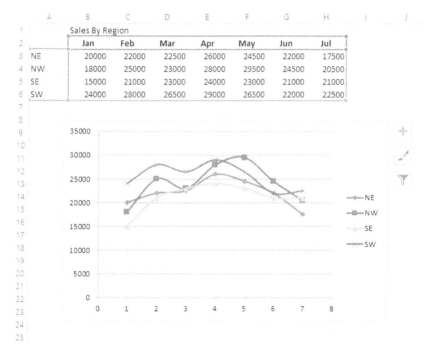

Step 3: Select the plus sign icon from the right side of the chart.

Step 4: Select the small arrow to the right of **Trendlines**.

Step 5: Select the type of trendline that you want to add from the list.

Step 6: If you did not select the specific data series and the chart has more than one, Excel displays a dialog box to help you choose the correct series.

Excel adds the Trendline.

Note that if you select **More Options** from the Trendline choices, Excel will open the Format Trendline pane, where you have several additional options for formatting your trendline.

Using Secondary Axes

To add a secondary vertical axis, use the following procedure.

Step 1: Select the chart.

Step 2: Select the **Chart Tools Format** tab.

Step 3: Select the Chart Elements box arrow and select the data series that you want to plot along a secondary vertical axis.

	Mar	Apr	May	Jun	Jul
	20	22500	26000	24500	22000	17500
NW	18000	25000	23000	28000	29500	24500	20500
SE	15000	21000	23000	24000	23000	21000	21000
SW	24000	28000	26500	29000	26500	22000	22500

Step 4: Select Format Selection from the Chart Tools Format tab on the Ribbon.

Step 5: Excel displays the Format Data Series pane. In the Format Data Series pane, select **Secondary Axis** under **Plot Series On**. The Format Data Series pane stays open so that you can format other aspects of the selected data series if desired.

In the following illustration, the chart type for the secondary axis has also been changed. With the secondary axis still selected, just go to the **Chart Tools Design** tab and select **Change Chart Type**.

In the Change Chart Type dialog box, your chart is automatically shown as a Custom Combination chart. You can use the drop down lists next to each data series to select another chart option for that data series.

Using Chart Templates

To save a chart as a template, use the following procedure.

Step 1: Right-click the chart.

Step 2: Select **Save As Template**.

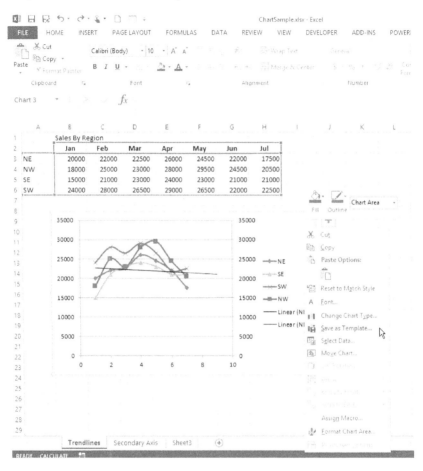

Step 3: In the Save Chart Template dialog box, enter a **File name** for the template.

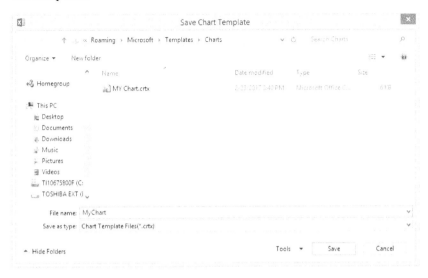

Step 4: Leave the file location as is, if you want the chart template to be available on the **Insert** tab when you select **Charts** or when you select **Change Chart Type**.

Step 5: Select **Save**.

To insert a chart based on their templates, use the following procedure.

Step 1: Select the data you want to use for your chart. You may want to copy the data from the Secondary Axis or Trendlines sheet in the sample file to Sheet 3 for this example.

Step 2: Select the **Insert** tab from the Ribbon.

Step 3: Select **Recommended Charts**.

Step 4: Select the **All Charts** tab.

Step 5: Select the **Templates** option from the left.

Step 6: Select the template that you have previously saved.

Step 7: Select **OK** to insert the chart.

Chapter 28 – Working with Slicers and Timelines

This chapter explains slicers and timelines. You will learn how to create a slicer in an existing table. You will also learn how to format a slicer. Finally, we will discuss how to disconnect or delete a slicer.

About Slicers and Timelines

Slicers were added in Excel2010 to filter PivotTable data. In Excel 2013, you can now use slicers to filter any table data. Slicers clearly indicate what data is shown in the table after you filter the data. They include buttons so that you can quickly filter data without having to use drop down lists to find the items you want to filter. Timelines are a type of slicer that is specific to date ranges.

A slicer typically displays the following elements:

- The slicer header – indicates the category of the items in the slicer.
- Unselected filtering button – indicates that the item is not included in the filter.
- Selected filtering button – indicates that the item is included in the filter.
- Clear Filter button – removes the filter by selecting all items in the slicer.
- A scroll bar – enables scrolling when there are more items than are currently visible in the slicer.
- Border moving and resizing controls – allow you to change the size and location of the slicer.

Using slicers

To filter your data, just select one or more of the buttons in the slicer.

You will likely that you will create more than once slicer to filter a data table or PivotTable report.

You can create a slicer that is associated with the current data table or PivotTable. You can also create a copy of a slicer.

Once you create a slicer, it appears on the worksheet alongside the table data, in a layered display if you have more than one. You can move or resize it as needed. Once created, a slicer can also be used with another table or PivotTable.

You can create slicers that work with the current data table or PivotTable or you can create a stand-alone slicer that can be associated with any other table at a later time. Stand-alone slicers can be referenced by Online Analytical Processing (OLAP) Cube functions.

Creating a Slicer in an Existing Table

To create a slicer in an existing table, use the following procedure.

Step 1: Place your cursor anywhere in the table.

Step 2: Select the **Insert** tab from the Ribbon.

Step 3: Select **Slicer**.

Step 4: In the Insert Slicers dialog box, select the check box(es) of the fields from the table for which you want to create a slicer.

290

Step 5: Select **OK**.

Step 6: To apply your filters, just select the buttons for the items you want to include. You can hold down the CTRL key while selecting to choose more than one button.

Formatting a Slicer

Note that when you select the slicer object, the **Slicer Tools Options** tab displays on the Ribbon, giving you additional tools to adjust your slicer settings, apply a new slicer style, or arrange and size the slicer object or the buttons.

To format a slicer, use the following procedure.

Step 1: Select the slicer that you want to format.

Step 2: Select the **Slicer Tools Options** tab from the Ribbon.

Step 3: You can select a new Style from the **Slicer Styles** area.

Step 4: Or, you can select the arrows next to **Slicer Styles** and select **New Slicer Style**.

Step 5: In the New Slicer Style dialog box, enter a **Name** for the new style.

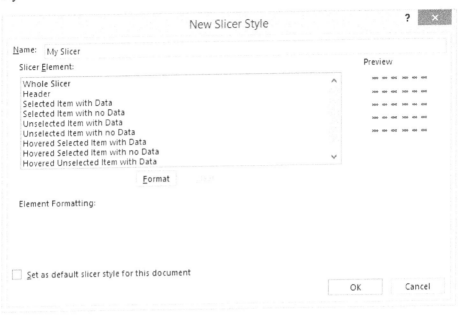

Step 6: Select the **Slicer Element** that you want to format from the list.

Step 7: Select **Format**. You can change the Font, Border, and Fill colors for each element.

Step 8: Select **OK** when you have finished formatting the selected element.

Step 9: Select **OK** when you have finished formatting all of the desired elements. You can check the **Set as default slicer quick style for this document** check box if desired.

Practice adjusting the size for the slicer and buttons as well.

Using a Timeline

To create a timeline in an existing table, use the following procedure.

Step 1: Place your cursor anywhere in the table.

Step 2: Select the **Insert** tab from the Ribbon.

Step 3: Select **Timeline**.

Step 4: In the Insert Timelines dialog box, select the check box(es) of the fields from the table for which you want to create a timeline.

Step 5: Select **OK**.

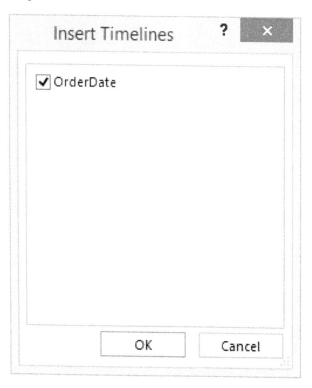

Step 6: Click a period on the timeline to include the date range you want to include in the PivotTable. You can also drag the edges of the timeline to expand the date range shown in the PivotTable. Remember that the timeline is interactive, so feel free to experiment.

OrderDate

All Periods   MONTHS

| 2011 |
| JN | JUL | AUG | SEP | OCT | NOV | DEC |

Step 7: You can change the period available in the slicer by clicking on the arrow next to the period shown (in this example, Months). Select a new period from the drop down list.

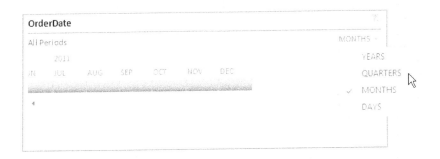

Review the Timeline Tools Options tab on the Ribbon and the Format Timeline pane. You can open the Format Timeline pane using the small square next to the Size group on the Timeline Tools Options tab on the Ribbon.

The Data Model in Excel 2013 is a new approach for integrating data from multiple tables. It actually builds a relational data source inside an Excel workbook, but it is virtually transparent. Data models provide the tabular data that is used in PivotTables, PivotCharts, and Power View reports. In this chapter, you will learn how to connect to a new external data source and create a PivotTable using an external data connection. You will use PivotTables to analyze data in multiple tables. You will also learn how to create relationships between tables.

Connecting to a New External Data Source

To connect to an external data source from an Access Database, use the following procedure.

Step 1: Select the **Data** tab from the Ribbon.

Step 2: Select **From Access.**

Step 3: In the Select Data Source dialog box, navigate to the location of the database you want to use and select **Open**.

Step 4: In the Select Table dialog box, check the box for the table to which you want to connect. If you would like to select more than one table or query, check the **Enable Selection of multiple tables** box. You will use multiple tables later in this chapter, so include more than one table.

Step 5: Select **OK**.

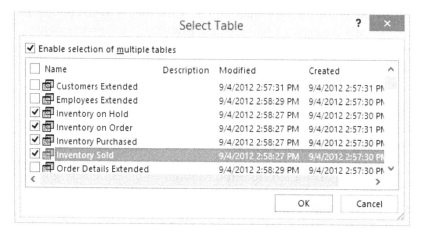

Step 6: In the Import Data dialog box, you can chose to create a connection only or a Table, PivotTable Report, PivotChart, or Power View Report. In this example, we will just create the connection.

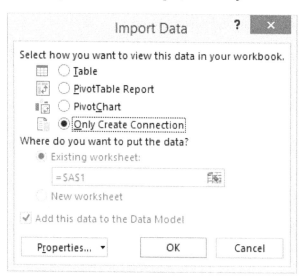

Creating a PivotTable Using an External Data Connection

 To create a PivotTable using an existing external data connection, use the following procedure.

Step 1: Select the Insert tab from the Ribbon.

Step 2: Select PivotTable.

Step 3: In the Create PivotTable dialog box, select Use an external data source.

Step 4: Select Choose Connection.

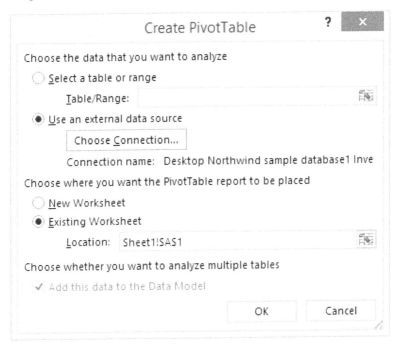

Step 5: In the Existing Connections dialog box, select the Connection that you want to use. You can use the **Show** drop down list to narrow the list of connections available.

Step 6: Select **Open**.

Step 7: In the Create PivotTable dialog box, choose where to place the new PivotTable.

Step 8: Select **OK**.

Excel adds an empty PivotTable and shows the Field pane so that you create the PivotTable you need.

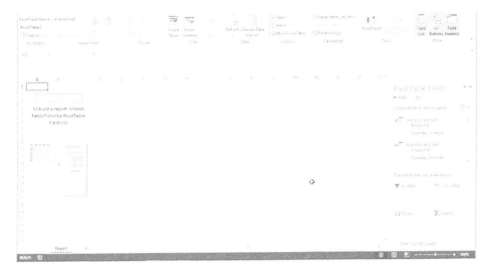

Working with PivotTables Based on Multiple Tables

A relationship matches data in two tables to create an association. Relationships allow you to use fields from multiple tables, even when the tables originate from different sources. Each table should have a meaningful name to help you identify them when creating the relationship.

One column in one of the tables should have unique, non-duplicate data values.

To work with the PivotTable Fields pane when the PivotTable is based on multiple tables (or a data connection with multiple tables).

Step 1: The Field pane contains all of the tables you selected when you imported the data. You can expand or compress the fields for each table by clicking on the plus or minus signs.

Step 2: Add the fields to the PivotTable report as you would for any PivotTable. You can add fields from any table to the VALUES, ROWS, or COLUMNS area.

303

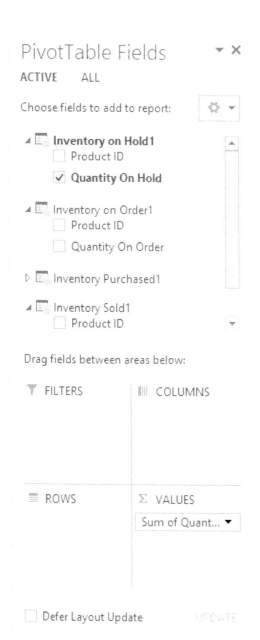

PivotTable Fields

ACTIVE   ALL

Choose fields to add to report:

▲ Inventory on Hold1
  ☐ Product ID
  ☑ **Quantity On Hold**

▲ Inventory on Order1
  ☐ Product ID
  ☐ Quantity On Order

▷ Inventory Purchased1

▲ Inventory Sold1
  ☐ Product ID

Drag fields between areas below:

▼ FILTERS   ‖‖ COLUMNS

≡ ROWS   Σ VALUES
                          Sum of Quant... ▼

☐ Defer Layout Update   UPDATE

304

Step 3: If you select fields from tables that are not already related, Excel displays the warning: Relationships between tables may be needed. Select **Create**.

Step 4: In the Create Relationship dialog box, select the first **Table** from the drop down list. In a one-to-many relationship, this table should be on the many side.

Step 5: Select the **Column** from that table to use in the relationship. This column should have unique values that match the values in the Related Column.

Step 6: Select the **Related Table** from the drop down list. This table should have at least one column of data that is related to the table you just selected.

Step 7: Select the **Column** from that table to use in the relationship from the drop down list.

Step 8: Select **OK**.

Chapter 30 – Working with Power View

Power View is an interactive way to explore, visualize, and present data that encourages ad-hoc reporting. This chapter will introduce you to Power View with lessons that include downloaded data from the Windows Azure Marketplace to learn how to create a Power View sheet, add additional tables to the data model used by the Power View Sheet and add an additional chart and change it to a map.

About Power View

Make sure that the PowerPivot Add-in is enabled, use the following procedure.

Step 1: Select the **File** tab to open the Backstage View.

Step 2: Select **Options**.

Step 3: Select **Add-ins**.

Step 4: From the **Manage** drop down list, select COM Add-ins.

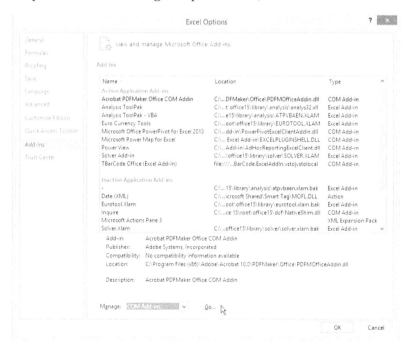

Step 5: Check the **Enable PowerPivot** box.

Step 6: Select **OK**.

Creating a Power View Sheet

To download the sample data, which creates a data model, use the following procedure.

Step 1: Select the **Power Pivot** tab from the Ribbon. You may need to restart Excel after enabling the Add-in.

Step 2: Select **Manage Data Model**.

Step 3: In the PowerPivot for Excel window, select **Get External Data**. Select **From Data Service**. Select **From Windows Azure Marketplace**.

Step 4: In the Table Import Wizard window, you can filter the list of options. To find the one for this lesson, select the following filters: **Free** and **Transportation and Navigation**.

Step 5: Next to **US Air Carrier Flight Delays**, select **Subscribe**.

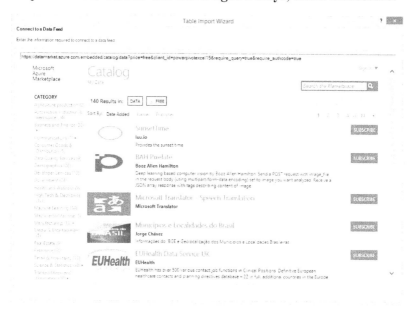

Step 6: Sign in with your Microsoft account. If necessary, create a Windows Azure Marketplace account. Continue making selections until you have finished subscribing to the information.

Step 7: At the end of the sample data, choose **Select Query**.

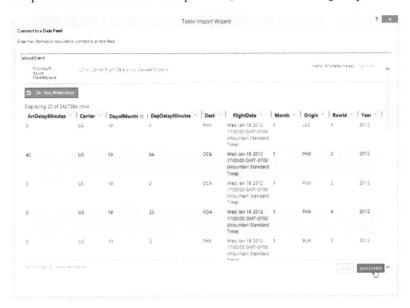

Step 8: You can change the name for the connection, if desired. Select **Next**.

Step 9: Select **Preview & Filter** from the Table Import Wizard.

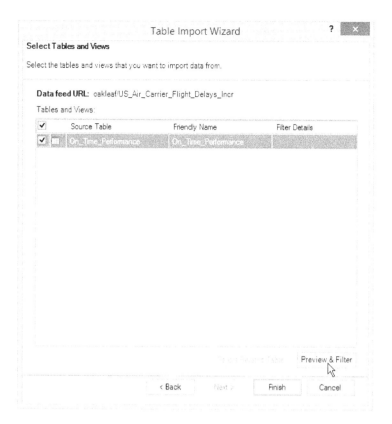

Step 10: Select **OK** to import all of the data. Select **Finish**. Be aware that this may take some time.

To create a Power View sheet, use the following procedure.

Step 1: Select the **Insert** tab from the Ribbon.

Step 2: Select **Power View Reports**.

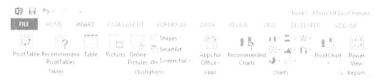

Now let us add some fields to the report.

Step 1: Expand the On_Time_Performance table.

Step 2: Check the **Carrier** box and the **ArrDelayMintues** box.

Step 3: In the **Values** box, select the arrow next to ArrDelayMinutes and select **Sum**. Now you have aggregates per carrier.

Now we will select a chart type.

Step 1: Select the **Design** tab from the Ribbon.

Step 2: Select **Column Chart**. Select **Clustered**.

Step 3: Let us add another field. In the **Field** list, drag DepDelayMinutes to the Values box under ArrDelayMinutes.

Notice that some carriers are better at on-time arrivals, while some are better at on-time departures.

Add a Table to the Data Model

To add a table to the data model, use the following procedure.

Step 1: Go to this site: **http://www.airfarewatchdog.com/pages/3799702/airline-letter-codes/**.

Step 2: Copy the two columns including the codes and the airline carrier names.

Step 3: On a blank worksheet in your workbook, enter the following headings in cell A1 and B1, respectively: AirlineCode and AirlineName

Step 4: In cell A2, paste the data you copied from the website.

Step 5: Format the data as a table.

Step 6: On the **Table Tools Design** tab, rename the table Airlines.

Step 7: Also rename the worksheet Airlines.

Now we will relate the tables in Power View, use the following procedure.

Step 1: Return to the Power View sheet.

Step 2: Your Airlines table should be in the Field list. If not, select **All** from the Field list.

Step 3: Select the column chart.

Step 4: Remove Carrier from the Axis box.

Step 5: Expand the Airlines tab to check the AirlineName box.

Excel displays the "Relationships between tables may be needed" message.

Step 6: Select **Create**.

Step 7: Select **Airlines** as the first table.

Step 8: Select **AirlineCode** as the column.

Step 9: Select **On_Time_Performance** as the second table.

Step 10: Select **Carrier** as the column.

Step 11: The message warning about the relationship just means that a primary key is created instead of a foreign key.

Step 12: Select **OK**.

To get the airport code data added to the data model, use the following procedure.

Step 1: Go to this site: **http://www.airportcodes.us/us-airports.htm**.

Step 2: Copy the four columns, including the code, name, city and state without the table heading.

Step 3: Add a new sheet to your workbook.

Step 4: Paste the data in cell A1.

Step 5: Rename the columns so that we can relate the data.

- Code = AirportCode

- Name = AirportName

- City = AirportCity

- State = AirportState

Step 6: Format the data as a table.

Step 7: On the **Table Tools Design** tab, rename the table **Airports**.

Step 8: Also rename the worksheet Airports.

Step 9: Return to the Power View sheet.

Step 10: Remove **Origin** from the Axis box.

Step 11: Expand the Airports table and check the **AirportName** box.

Step 12: Select **Create** in the message to create the appropriate relationships.

Step 13: Select **Airports** as the first table.

Step 14: Select **AirportCode** as the column.

Step 15: Select **On_Time_Performance** as the related table.

Step 16: Select **Origin** as the column.

Step 17: Select **OK**.

Adding a Map to a Power View Report

To create another chart, use the following procedure.

Step 1: You can start another visualization not related to your current fields by clicking on the blank area outside the previous chart.

Step 2: In the Field list, on the On_Time_Performance table, check the Origin box. Also check the DepDelayMinutes box.

Step 3: Select the arrow next to DepDelayMinutes and select Average.

Step 4: Let us decrease the decimal for that column. Click on the column and use the Decrease Decimal tool on the Design tab of the Ribbon.

Step 5: Now let us convert this table to a bar chart. Select Bar Chart from the Design tab on the Ribbon. Select Stacked Bar.

Step 6: You can move and resize the chart to maximize what you can see with the available real estate on the sheet.

To create a map, use the following procedure.

Step 1: Select the Airports chart.

Step 2: Select the Design tab from the Ribbon.

Step 3: Select Map.

Step 4: If Power View puts AirportName in the Color box, drag it to the Locations box.

Step 5: Select the plus sign in the upper right corner of the map to zoom in. Use the cursor to reposition the map.

To filter the map, use the following procedure.

Step 1: Select the map.

Step 2: In the Filters area, select Map.

Step 3: Select Average of DepDelayMinutes.

Step 4: Drag the left side of the scroll bar to show only delays that are greater than 10 minutes.

Additional Titles

The Technical Skill Builder series of books covers a variety of technical application skills. For the availability of titles please see https://www.silvercitypublications.com/shop/. Note the Master Class volume contains the Essentials, Advanced, and Expert (when available) editions.

Current Titles

Microsoft Excel 2013 Essentials

Microsoft Excel 2013 Advanced

Microsoft Excel 2013 Expert

Microsoft Excel 2013 Master Class

Microsoft Word 2013 Essentials

Microsoft Word 2013 Advanced

Microsoft Word 2013 Expert

Microsoft Word 2013 Master Class

Microsoft Project 2010 Essentials

Microsoft Project 2010 Advanced

Microsoft Project 2010 Expert

Microsoft Project 2010 Master Class

Microsoft Visio 2010 Essentials

Microsoft Visio 2010 Advanced

Microsoft Visio 2010 Master Class

Coming Soon

Microsoft Access 2013 Essentials

Microsoft Access 2013 Advanced

Microsoft Access 2013 Expert

Microsoft Access 2013 Master Class

Microsoft PowerPoint 2013 Essentials

Microsoft PowerPoint 2013 Advanced

Microsoft PowerPoint 2013 Expert

Microsoft PowerPoint 2013 Master Class

Microsoft Outlook 2013 Essentials

Microsoft Outlook 2013 Advanced

Microsoft Outlook 2013 Expert

Microsoft Outlook 2013 Master Class

Microsoft Publisher 2013 Essentials

Microsoft Publisher 2013 Advanced

Microsoft Publisher 2013 Master Class

Windows 7 Essentials

Windows 8 Essentials

www.ingramcontent.com/pod-product-compliance
Lightning Source LLC
Chambersburg PA
CBHW071104050326
40690CB00008B/1106